Enough Dreaming

Business Ownership Is Yours for the Taking

Andrew Cremé

Enough Dreaming, Business Ownership is Your for the Taking

A McKinney Publishing Production

Printing history: First Edition, November 2016

Copyright © 2016 by Andrew Cremé

All rights reserved

This book, or parts thereof, may not be reproduced in any form without permission.

For information address:

McKinney Publishing

11625 Custer Rd. Suite 110-501

Frisco, TX 75035

Visit our website at:

WWW.McKinneyPublishing.com

ISBN: 978-1-943518-11-1

Printed in the United States of America

Acknowledgments

For my loving wife Janelle, who put up with my long hours and ceaseless work in order to build a business. And for my daughter Gianna, who inspires me to be a better man everyday.

Contents

Getting Started 7
Business Plan 18
Defining a Business 40
Operational Management 49
Business Image 84
Strategic Management 90
Growth Strategies 97
Exit Strategies 105
Summary 108
Index 110

Getting Started

You may be reading this wanting to be an entrepreneur. Some of you might have already begun the journey and are wondering where improvements can be made. There are many things that make entrepreneurship appealing to the masses. These include such ideas as holding your own destiny in your hands, creating something that contributes to society, potentially having more job security, and being able to prove your worth to the world through your customers instead of to a boss or even a human resources associate if you are in the job seeking stage. On the other hand, there are many things that people believe of entrepreneurs that just aren't true: that you can make your own hours, that it offers more flexibility than working for someone else, and that it's the easy way out of having to find a job. Being an entrepreneur is a grueling profession that offers long hours, being on call constantly, and very little forgiveness when mistakes occur. You have to quickly become a well-seasoned CEO, Senior HR Executive, and Top Sales Associate in an extremely short time frame. But if you have the drive and the spark to make it work, it is a great way to both earn a living and grow professionally.

What does it take to be an entrepreneur? Many believe that it takes a lot of up-front capital, a large network, and an established skill set, but that would be wrong. While those are helpful, what it takes predominately to be an entrepreneur is a thirst for knowledge, an eye for opportunity, and the courage to fail and get knocked down yet still get up and keep going.

There are so many businesses already out there, and finding the right space to compete in can be a bit intimidating. As I mentioned, having an eye for opportunity definitely required. One of the best ways to train yourself to see the opportunities that exist is to use a framework, or a systematic structure to evaluate the possibilities that are all around. Lets consider the most common method, but also quickly move to a more expanded view.

Mousetrap 2.0

A basic mousetrap is frequently used as an example for entrepreneurship because it is simple and fits the situation very well. Let's look at using the business as a mousetrap in these first basic examples.

1) New Mousetrap in a New Market. Perhaps you decide to go in a completely different direction and make an oversized mousetrap that not only traps mice but also traps opossums, rats, squirrels, bugs - or perhaps a trapping *service* instead of a product. That's all new mousetrap in a new market thinking.

2) Upgraded Mousetrap in the Same Market. You could decide to build an upgraded model of a mousetrap that targets cruelty free markets of people who don't want to harm mice in their removal or perhaps one that is more intricate and exterminates the smarter than average mouse. Again, there is always the service equivalent where you offer a trapping service of an animal and take the same strategic path.

3) Same Mousetrap in the Same Market. Sounds like the hardest path to take, but this is probably done more than the other two combined. If you take this path, you have to have something that differentiates your product in other ways – it looks better, you have a better price, you make it more accessible, or perhaps it's your customer service that you focus on with vendor and customer relations.

BASIC TYPES OF MOUSETRAPS

1
- New Mousetrap
- New Market

2
- Upgraded Mousetrap
- Same Market

3
- Same Mousetrap
- Same Market

Enough Dreaming

I believe the basic mousetrap models of creating a business are the most common, but there are a few more to mention for the extra creative people out there. Maybe you have an idea of what you want to do but aren't quite sure how to get over that hump that turns an idea into a business. The following exercise is what helps me constantly when I am needing a more systematic way to be creative.

The best way to think about markets and services is that – "There is some product or service I want to offer to some population of people" and the only factor that really comes into consideration is the type of business. It is seriously that simple. That's why there are so many successful "serial entrepreneurs". Because once you get this type of thinking down you'll be able to turn any idea into a business in no time.

Getting Started

EXPANDED STRATEGY OF MOUSETRAPS

I want you to relook at that diagram because, yes, it is seriously that easy to come up with a strategic concept on a business idea. You really don't need a whole book about dreaming to figure out what you can do – you just need an industry. On the next pages are a few examples.

HEALTH AND FITNESS BUSINESS STRATEGY IDEAS

These health and fitness strategy ideas might be the result of using the expanded strategy of mousetraps concept to think about some different markets or different application ideas within that industry. We can also look at the automotive industry for another example.

Getting Started

AUTOMOTIVE BUSINESS STRATEGY IDEAS

If you look at this automotive model closely, you can see ideas that are developing in the market and have developed in the market already. People sell their cars on websites like autotrader.com everyday by purchasing an ad. They also go to places like CarMax and sell their cars outright without having to purchase anything in return. I have even seen people who specialize in finding certain cars for

Enough Dreaming

people and doing the deal for them, as well as off-road vehicle sale dealerships. From the automotive grid, the only remaining options left undeveloped are companies that offer to sell your car for you for a commission, or some sort of official car-swap website. Such options very well might exist already and I don't even realize it. What other options come to mind for you? What combinations suggest a possible improvement?

The bottom line, when it comes to mousetraps and the idea of starting your own business, is that there are multiple models. You can build a new mousetrap in a new market –like Google, Apple, and Facebook did; you can build an improved upon mousetrap in an existing market – like Amazon, Whole Foods, and Netflix did; or you can build an established mousetrap in an established market and enter competitive markets like many small businesses – doctors' offices, lawn care companies, and insurance agencies, to name just a few.

Another common way that people build new mousetraps in new markets is through knowledge or experience, where the product is a service rather than a commodity (as in the prior example of selling a car for someone else online). These days, especially, many opportunities come through specialized expertise in technology and technology development through websites, applications, and programs. It is possible to start a business around a specialized area without the practical know-how to do it oneself; but that requires either a partnership with someone who can do the bulk of the work or starting capital to hire people with the expertise that is needed.

The most common way that people are inspired to build new mousetraps is by working in an existing market and feeling that there is an opportunity to improve on a function of that job. This improvement may even turn into a business in itself. For example, a purchasing manager for an electronics business might have a problem with the cost of continually getting updates on production statuses overseas. If they had the desire to do so, they might work on a technology that automatically uploads the progression based on container weights and will show the progress on a website. That system could be sold independently of the electronics business to all companies that have manufacturing process frustrations.

As someone who worked predominately in the medical field, I often came upon opportunities for this second type of mousetrap. Many doctors' offices had problems with patients forgetting about their appointments, and they didn't have time to call every patient beforehand to confirm the appointment. Their only other option at the time was to use software that required their office staff to enter in the times of appointments for each patient and an automated system would call the patients with a robotic reminder. While this helped some of the no-show rates, it often occurred to me that the best option would be a call center, with remote access to their scheduling system, where staff would log in and make personal calls to the patients and have the ability to reschedule them to different times if the current appointment time was no longer convenient.

Another mousetrap idea that came about while I was building my first business revolved around the idea of networking. Networking is one of the most time intensive aspects of building a business, and it takes time to properly vet and screen business partners appropriately. Instead of meeting with people one by one, it seemed to me that someone should be able to form associations within different markets that take all the screening upon themselves. So for a medical based association, you would have members who represent all the service providers a physician might need – a banker, lawyer, accountant, printer, advertising agent, supplier, medical equipment rep, a physician recruiter, etc. People develop these networks over time, but by forming an association, a new business would be able to jump start their work, and existing members would solidify their referrals and standing within that industry.

Most new businesses, however, typically fit into the third mousetrap category of an established business in an established market.

Enough Dreaming

For many people who want to run a business and are willing to try to outwork the competition, this can be a great option. All franchises fall into this category as well as most professional careers such as being a doctor, lawyer, accountant, or even most consultants. What is very appealing to many people about this model, as well, is that it gives people an opportunity to create more income for their households while maintaining full time jobs. A janitor at a school that drives an old pickup can easily start a lawn service with his lawn mower, or start a handyman service with his tools, after his day job ends and on weekends. Often these "side jobs" are great launching pads for people who want to get out of dead-end jobs and enter entrepreneurship once they can make enough money on their side business to support themselves full time.

Do you have to be involved in the tech space to build a new mousetrap in a new market? No, but you do need to know and read about technologies in order to understand how they can potentially be adapted by a marketplace. Just like you don't have to already work in a certain business in order to build an improved mousetrap in that existing market, but you do need to talk to the people who perform those jobs to understand their frustrations. This can be as simple as joining community groups or simply speaking in more detail to family and friends to develop your first idea. And do you need to have capital or equipment in order to build a competing mousetrap in an existing market? Again the answer is no. If your current job is, for example, in sales, you could start a business giving sales seminars to small business owners (and build your network at the same time). Or if you want to do lawn care but don't own the equipment, you might be able to find someone who will loan you their lawnmower in exchange for an agreement to mow their lawn with an additional promise of a rental fee that would be due at some future date.

What this all circles back around to is the need to be a knowledge seeker, to see an opportunity when it's in front of you, and to have the drive to make it work even if it means you might fail the first time around. Take the time to learn from your friends, family, and from as much literature as you can find. Eventually you will have that "aha" moment where you begin to discover what the market you would like to enter truly involves and just what kind of mousetrap you need to develop: one that fits an existing market, one that improves on an existing market, or one that creates a new market from your product or service.

Business Plan

A business plan is a tool used by both existing and new businesses to define their businesses and examine the markets to decide the best way to move forward with growth. Because business plans can be time consuming, many businesses forgo their creation. This, however, is a big mistake. By creating a business plan, especially for a new business, you are basically trading time for a supercharger to your business growth engine. Yes, you might not start as soon as you'd like, but once you begin you will quickly find your competitors in your rear view mirror because they won't be as laser focused in their efforts.

Professional business plans are robust documents that include the following: executive summary, mission, vision, core values, situational analysis, known risks, market analysis, demographic report, SWOT analysis, competitive analysis, strategic overview, business objectives, product and service strategy, pricing strategy, promotional strategy, channel strategy, internal marketing strategy, marketing plan, budget review, financial pro-forma, exit plan, and conclusion. Let's look at an example of a scaled down version of a professional business plan for a fictitious coffee shop that someone may want to open.

Detailed Business Plan Example
The Triple Roast Coffee Shop

Executive Summary:

Beginning in the third quarter of 2017, Brown Bean Enterprises (BBE) will open The Triple Roast – a coffee entertainment venue. While the coffee space itself is overrun by mega-chains and small pastry shops that are expanding their coffee menus, BBE believes that by offering a quality product, with a small retail footprint, and a versatile business model, they can differentiate their business and brand from others. The name Triple Roast was chosen as a play on terms and association when it comes to the model. Not only will the store be a traditional coffee shop that offers inside and outside service, it closes that model at 5pm when it will become more of a public entertainment venue, especially on the weekends. Lastly, there will be a catering model that offers a morale boosting experience to businesses where they can have their own barista for a morning.

Mission:

To Innovate Coffee One Cup Served at a Time

Vision:

To partially redefine the word "coffee shop"

Enough Dreaming

Core Values:

<u>To be Tactical</u> – Know Your Customer's Needs and Meet them 100% of the Time

<u>To be Strategic</u> – Constantly Look for Ways to Innovate

<u>To be Effective</u> – Know Your Strengths and Stay Close to Them

<u>To have Fun</u> – Wake People Up with a Smile and Close the Day with a Grin

Situational Analysis:

Jack Pappas, a business executive with over 15 years in the retail management and business service space has always had a passion for coffee and helping people. On a family vacation one year, Jack noticed a retail shopping center with three businesses that happened to be right next to each other – a traditional coffee shop, a ballet studio, and a small Chinese take-out restaurant. Suddenly it dawned on him that these type of businesses could all be merged into one amazing coffee experience. A place where you get your morning coffee in the morning, go to meet with a business acquaintance in the afternoon, and wrap up the day with a friend at a comedy show with liquored coffee drinks.

Because Jack doesn't have a background in making or serving coffee that didn't come out of his french press, he figured that the best way to begin is by way of a coffee "food" truck. This would allow him to develop the skills necessary to understand the coffee business as to how to source his product, develop equipment knowledge, and most importantly, develop a customer base that will eventually be so loyal as to follow him (if not literally, then at least on social media).

Risks:

Because the business proposed has two distinct phases, there is a significant difference between the short-term risks and long-term risks. The short-term risks are relatively minimal to get started due to the healthy market for used food service equipment as well as used food-trucks. The only major risks at first revolve around learning the trade of preparing coffee and getting new customers.

The long-term risks are much greater than the short-term. Because the business model Jack is proposing is unique and has a presence in multiple venues, it also increases the number of competitors. What is excellent about the rollout, however, is that the business has to succeed short-term in order to make it to long-term. That will mean that the company at this time will have three possible routes to take: 1) continue along to the new brick and mortar plan, 2) forget the brick and mortar and just expand the now cash-flush coffee truck business, or 3) do both.

Market Analysis:

Food trucks are best known for operating out of a downtown environment where significant money can be saved by not getting into a retail space and it is convenient for busy workers to get coffee before starting their day. Permitting will be the biggest obstacle when planning out location sites. If the chosen city has public transportation, there may also be opportunity to set up shop in a convenient location where people are naturally waiting to head to their jobs.

Demographic Report:

An average purchase by customers will range between five and seven dollars, and coffee drinkers are known to make this purchase every day of the work week, or five times a week. Five times a week multiplied by five dollars averages $100 per month or $1200 per year. Assuming most people will not spend more than 5 percent of their after-tax income on coffee, our target demographic would be individuals with an income of around $40,000, or a household income of $80,000

SWOT Analysis:

(S) Strengths

Passion

Intense Focus

Great Staff

Executive business experience and knowledge

(W) Weaknesses

Single Location

Poor Cash Flow

Unproven Business Model

(O) Opportunities

No Direct Model Competitors

In-Demand Product

Upward Financial Mobility of Market

(T) Threats

Many Alternative Model Competitors

Permitting Regulation

Weather Deterrence

Competitive Analysis:

Coffee Shops – While these are the most direct competitors, there are many weaknesses that they have that can be exploited. They are known for their higher pricing models, long lines, and lack of customer service. Also, because they are in fixed locations, if it isn't convenient for customers in the morning, they are frequently forgone.

Donut Shops – Depending on the area, these can also be commonly found. Major chains have been shown to have abysmally long wait times and extreme poor customer service with mediocre food products that are inherently unhealthy. Also, because they are in fixed locations, if it isn't convenient for customers in the morning, they are frequently forgone.

Gas Stations – These tend to cater to people in a lower income bracket due to their plain coffee selections and are most successful in areas where there is extreme automobile commuting.

Strategy:

In order to compete in this market, given the competitors, the highest likelihood of success would be in a location with a strong downtown market with ample permitting options. People who forgo stopping on their way and drink their own coffee in their car may consider purchasing another cup or a food item once they have reached their destination and have time to wait in a line or have time to kill by waiting at public transportation stops such as train or subway parking lots.

Objectives:

Being a start-up, the primary objective is to prove the business model as quickly and efficiently as possible. Having multiple options to test would be the best way to figure out which is the best place to station the coffee food truck and at what times. A secondary objective will be to minimize downtime by having a strategy that maximized truck usage during nontraditional hours. Setting up arrangements with larger companies to park the truck in their parking lots during the afternoon for afternoon coffee runs or having some select lunch items available for sale would be advantageous. Also, tapping into sales reps that have budgets to bring coffees to customers would be a symbiotic relationship so they don't have to take the time to get the coffee from a distant coffee shop.

Product Service Strategy:

Countering the barriers of the industry such as long wait times, poor customer service, and unhealthy food options would all be product service strategies. We can counter the long wait times as best as possible by having the most time efficient equipment that creates the drink of choice wanted in as little of time as possible. Also, having a limited healthy menu that focuses on pre-cut fruit, soft-boiled eggs, and a possibly one hot item such as a chicken sandwich would also help cut down on having to work with the staff on more processes.

Developing an online app for a smartphone could be a good way to allow people to preorder their items and have them ready with a fast-track line. And of course hiring the right people who are pleasant yet competent is the best way to combat poor customer service.

Pricing Strategy:

All items sold will have to be cost accounted for in order to guarantee a healthy margin on every purchase. Focusing on items that can be purchased in bulk such as a single type of coffee bean and food items that can be frozen will help keep pricing variability from creeping into the equation. Until sales have been established, exact pricing on food and menu items will be difficult at first, but it will be better to overstock wherever possible so sales are not lost in the process.

Promotion Strategy:

Promotion will be key in kicking off this business. Once locations have been set for test points, all businesses in the area and their staff will be notified about the convenient service now located nearby. If the truck is to be parked in commuter lots, informational flyers can be left on the cars letting them know what they can purchase from the coffee food truck and the hours available.

As mentioned before, an online app as well as social media will be important to develop to create a following of customers. Because the service is mobile, people should be able to know where it is, how to order in advance, and also provide fun content online to keep people engaged and hopefully create some word-of-mouth buzz.

Lastly, there can be niche strategies such as promotional business pricing to select businesses to encourage their employees to purchase from the truck. And perhaps there are other messaging options to consider such as "going green" and having all biodegradable products used or offering vegetarian or vegan options. Fair trade coffee is also a considerable moral issue that people may relate with or pass others by just to know their money is being used in supporting small farmers instead of large corporations. The same goes for using local farmers markets for fruit instead of grocery chains.

Channel Strategy:

Primary channel strategy will be location placement between the hours of 6:30 am and 10 am for walk-up traffic. Secondary channel strategy will be contacts with large businesses in the area with dedicated parking lots where either a discount can be offered or a "rent-a-barista" program can be offered within the office during non-peak hours. A tertiary channel strategy will be around maximum lunchtime utilization which will be the most difficult as there are other established and dedicated food trucks in this space already.

Service based Internal Marketing:

Other than self-serve coffee stations such as in gas stations, there is an inherent wait time built into the ordering process. Our staff will begin internally marketing to customers by handing out brief survey cards that can be completed within 15 seconds while they wait for their orders. On these, we will collect not only valuable customer feedback, but hopefully also email addresses that will allow us to launch a social media platform and online app platform much faster.

As a reward for customer participation and engagement, promotions will be offered such as free food or coffee as well as priority ordering with loyalty points.

External Marketing

External marketing will be done in the second phase of marketing due to cost restrictions. Direct mail postcards can be sent to targeted zip-codes where people are known to have the appropriate amount of household income to be interested. Also, advertisements can be run in community-based publications where people may utilize public transportation parking lots or are known to work in the downtown area.

Flyers will be created that explain the service and ask people to sign up for email or text promotions which can be handed out to customers as well as local businesses that surround the areas where the coffee food truck will be located during peak hours. A separate flyer will be created specifically for businesses that advertise the "rent-a-barista" program.

All social media platforms that are appropriate will be created and utilized to the max at the start - such as Facebook, Twitter, Instagram, and Snapchat. These will be used concurrently with the online app developed over time once the marketing budget has been set aside. Also, a basic website will also be created right away to advertise the menu, as well as services, to businesses and the mission and purpose of the business for relatability by the customer.

Internal Marketing

The primary internal marketing strategy will revolve around collecting survey cards from customers with their emails to begin to develop a database. These emails can also be used in a promotional "refer-a-friend" program in which friend referrals merit a free drink upgrade and earn loyalty points to have fast track orders.

MARKETING PLAN:

Phase	Action	Description	Owner
Prelaunch	Surveys	Ask patrons for feedback on possible truck sites during peak hours	Jack
First	Survey Cards	15 Second Surveys to gain some information and emails	Lisa
Second	Website	Create basic website and business cards	Jack
Third	Business Flyers	Flyers handed out to businesses promoting barista rental	Jack
Fourth	Email Campaign	Begin Customer engagement by using emails to send newsletter with promotion	Jack
Fifth	Social Media	Develop social media platforms to engage customer base and move away from email marketing	Jack

Business Plan Example

FLIGHT PLAN:

Phase	Action	Completion Date	Cost
Prelaunch	Surveys	Sep. 1	$200
First	Survey Cards	Oct. 30	$400
Second	Website	Dec. 1	$1500
Third	Business Flyers	Dec. 1	$400
Fourth	Email Campaign	Dec. 31	$50
Fifth	Social Media	Feb 1	$10

Financials:

The research performed shows that we should be able to supply the coffee food truck with all food, coffee beans, cups, sugars, and "product" for 15% of our gross revenue over time. What we are aiming for are industry best practices that show another 15% should be going to the owner or investors at the end of the year, which at this point would most likely be reinvested into the business. That leaves our net cost-of-good-sold and projected project operating budget as 70%.

In order to keep lines moving quickly, Jack's neighbor Lisa has agreed to come on part time to help get her out of her current coffee shop job, but to still provide the flexibility she is looking for during non-peak hours to take care of her toddler at home. Her cost is $15 per hour and he is expecting to need her for five hours per day for five days a week totaling $375 per week or $1500 per month based on a four-week month.

Enough Dreaming

The equipment needed to make the coffee as quickly as possible plus other equipment, a POS (Point of Sale) System to take payments, as well as the truck payment itself all add up to $1200 per month. And Jack needs to keep his lights on at home and pay his basics so he will draw a $3,000 per month salary. Everything combined so far will look as follows:

Staffing	$4,500/month	$1,125/week	$77 per "peak" hour
Marketing	$450/month	$112.50/week	$7.50 per "peak" hour
Equipment & Truck	$1,200/month	$300/week	$20 per "peak" hour
Est. Cost of Goods Sold	$1,325/month	$331.25/week	$22.10 per "peak" hour
Expected profit	$1,325/month	$331.25/week	$22.10 per "peak" hour

Adding everything together on an hourly basis and working with industry best practice data, we know that the true operating costs per hour are approximately $150 per hour. At an average of $5 per purchase that means the company needs 30 people to visit their coffee food truck every hour. That is a 2-minute turn-around time on an order which will mean the prices might need to be slightly higher, hours might have to be extended, or the ancillary services such as "rent-a-barista" may have to be factored in. What also may play into this equation is that Jack has 6 months of expenses set aside from his former job and he might have to tap into that to keep the business afloat while he discovers what works and what doesn't work.

Exit Plan:

The exit plans for this temporary business model of the coffee food truck are multiple. The first option would be to get the company to a good profitability and then to sell it off with the option to reinvest the money into the initial brick and mortar idea. If reinvestment is the goal and not just to make a one-time profit, retaining the brand would be the best way to go in order to retain as many customers are possible. A second exit plan would be to retain the original coffee food truck and use the financial and operational data to expand that line by franchising it to other entrepreneurs in other markets. By doing this, Jack wouldn't receive the initial influx of money provided by a sale, but could use the cash flow provided by the truck as well as any franchise fees received residually.

A third exit plan isn't so much of an exit plan but an expansion plan. The original goal was to have a business with three operational lines – coffee shop, dance studio, and a take-out restaurant. Once the truck is cash flowing on its own, it would be plausible to expand into one of these other areas on a part-time basis. The truck could be outfitted with additional equipment that allows it to cook dinner food which people could order to either be picked up or delivered, or a small space could be rented part-time to begin organizing the dance studio model and begin developing a list of customers. The truck could be used to promote either one of these two models to help jump-start them while savings are accumulated for a full transition.

Conclusion:

Jack Pappas has a dream to revolutionize the coffee shop experience by being innovative with its application and adding on additional services so it isn't underutilized. The practical first step in doing so and the one that takes the least amount of up-front capital

Enough Dreaming

is creating a coffee-based food truck that could service as a pilot program and a step into understanding the core competency of his business which is serving quality coffee drinks in an efficient and pleasant manner. By taking a small step in this direction instead of jumping with both feet into an unproven business model, it reduces the risk involved while ensuring attainment of the key core competency and gaining a financially profitable business in as little time as possible.

Business Plan Breakdown

As you can see by the prior detailed example, business planning is a large and complicated area to cover and, while it can seem intimidating at first, you can get the hang of it in no time. But luckily for you, for many basic start-ups we can focus on an abbreviated version of a business plan, which is simpler and more manageable for you to achieve. We will cover this type of business plan in the coming section and explain why we do what we do.

Business plans are great tools to organize thoughts on a business and put together a well thought out strategy. These plans can range from a full review of existing operations, including a growth plan and an investment segment; however, for the purpose of this book, we will be focusing on simple business plans that anyone can do with some time on their hands. While these will provide vision and strategy to the company, business plans are continuously evolving and should be updated and revamped every few years to incorporate growth or changes in the market environment or business structure.

Creating a business plan can truly separate two start-up businesses, helping one succeed where the other may fail. For example, let's say that both Robert and Michael are planning on starting a law firm right out of law school. Robert took the time to map out a business plan while Michael was eager to begin and hung his shingle right away. While completing his business plan, Robert was able to determine that right by his house there were 25 attorneys actively practicing all areas of the law, but on the outskirts of town there were only 3 practicing attorneys. Robert also discovered that around the outskirts of town, the predominant occupation of households worked in the agricultural field. Instead of opening his practice right away, Robert decided the commute was worth it and opened his practice in the outskirts of town. There he decided to niche his practice in the areas of employment, environmental, and agricultural regulatory law. By going around to the local farmers and getting involved in the 4H programs with his family, he was able to build a robust practice in no time. Michael, on the other hand, was living hand to mouth for months while he competed in the hardest area of town against lawyers with robust networks and stellar reputations. This occurs every day throughout the world, all because one person took the time to get to know the soil before they planted by creating a business plan where the other person did not.

Let's take a look at another example for how to start a business plan in a common area – lawn care. The formation of a good business plan starts by answering a certain number of generalized questions:

- *What is the business going to do?*
- *What equipment will be needed and how will that be acquired?*
- *How much will you charge for your services?*
- *Who else is currently competing in the same area?*
- *How will you gain new customers?*
- *As you get income, where will it be allocated?*

Enough Dreaming

What is the business going to do?

The business will have a general goal of providing people in a certain geographic area quality and reliable lawn services.

What equipment will be needed and how will that be acquired?

You will need a hand mower, a weed eater, and a vehicle to transport them in.

How much will you charge for your services?

You will charge $15 per week for a small lawn, $25 per week for a medium lawn, and $50 per week for a large lawn with a six-month contract or 20% higher for a month-to-month contract. These prices can be figured out by asking around at local lawn companies, by asking neighbors what they pay, or by making cold calls or visits to communities and asking them if they don't mind saying what they are paying because you are starting a business and would like to benchmark the market. This last tactic is especially fruitful because it allows you to follow up with a quote on their lawn once you are operational.

Who else is currently competing in the same area?

You can tell who is competing in this space by both going online to see who is listed there as well as by driving around and jotting down the names as you see them on the sides of trucks.

How will you gain new customers?

In order to gain new customers you can begin, as many people do, by asking family and friends who live nearby if you can do their lawns (but you should always be proactive in making sure you are exceeding their expectations or you might damage a relationship). You can also keep costs low by continuing to go door to door to market to people and shake their hand and let them know you are available in the future if they ever become dissatisfied with their current lawn service providers.

As you get income, where will it be allocated?

A very important part of the business plan is knowing where your money is going to be spent or distributed as it comes in. I prefer to set income as a percentage of services instead of a flat rate because a) it keeps you motivated to continuously produce, and b) it allows you to start thinking of reinvesting profits for the sake of growth from the very first dollar. So let's say that you are going to apply 50% to salaries and 40% to reinvestment. You can then list the items that will create capacity for you as you grow – for example: a couple gas cans, a riding lawn mower, a trailer, etc. You will also need to set aside some money (10%) for emergency repairs since you need to have working equipment to get paid. Once you know this, you can begin to put together financial estimates.

Financial Example of Equipment, Capacity, Cost, and Income:

Lawn Equipment	Cost vs Income
A Hand Mower and a Weed Wacker Capacity: 5 Lawns @ $25	Reinvestment Cost: $0 Total Income Per Day: $125
A Hand Mower, a Weed Wacker, and a Gas Can Capacity: 6 Lawns @ $25	Reinvestment Cost: $25 Total Income Per Day: $150
A Hand Mower, a Weed Wacker, and Two Gas Cans Capacity: 6 Lawns @ $25 1 Lawn @ $15	Reinvestment Cost: $50 Total Income Per Day: $165
A Riding Mower, A Hand Mower, a Weed Wacker, and Two Gas Cans Capacity: 13 Lawns @ $25	Reinvestment Cost: $1550 Total Income Per Day: $325
A Riding Mower, A Hand Mower, a Weed Wacker, and Three Gas Cans Capacity: 15 Lawns @ $25	Reinvestment Cost: $1575 Total Income Per Day: $375
A Riding Mower, A Hand Mower, a Weed Wacker, and Four Gas Cans Capacity: 15 Lawns @ $25 1 Lawn @ 15	Reinvestment Cost: $1600 Total Income Per Day: $390

If you are going to work really hard to grow this new business and commit to 7 days a week, you should have the opportunity to make $125 per day or $875 per week to start. Your total commitment goal should be towards getting 35 lawns to mow during the course of a week with the current equipment. At this rate you can reinvest $350 into the business to get faster equipment to do more in a little over a month. In the final scenario listed with a riding mower, a hand mower, a weed whacker, and four gas cans you will have the ability to make $2,730 per week at $390 per day. You would put aside $1,092 aside of this to be able to buy nicer and more efficient equipment as it breaks instead of fixing it, and eventually use these profits to also hire other people to do lawns simultaneously – creating even more capacity.

Once again, the questions to ask when creating simple business plan are:

- *What is the business going to do?*
- *What equipment will be needed and how will that be acquired?*
- *How much will you charge for your services?*
- *Who else is currently competing in the same area?*
- *How will you gain new customers?*
- *As you get income, where will it be allocated?*

To these we add:

- *What feeder services currently exist?*

What feeder services currently exist?

Last, but not least, you should also be on the constant lookout for what feeder services exist in your market. What I mean by this is what other businesses exist that have the ability to give or take away business from you. This is a time to really brainstorm and

Enough Dreaming

think out of the box. Obviously lawn care might be promoted by tree trimming services, but what about pest control also? Perhaps it could be something that may not be so obvious – such as plumbers or people who work on irrigation systems or wells? It might be from dog trainers who come to perspective clients' houses, or cable repairmen who need to run wires through the grass or past the bushes. Knowing what feeder services exist in a market provides the opportunity to either develop mutually beneficial relationships with companies that you refer business back and forth with, or it gives you opportunities to expand in the future.

Mapping out industry feeder services is one of the most underutilized areas of business growth. In order to demonstrate this let's consider two new house-cleaning businesses. Mary's house cleaning business has only one concern in growing her business – doing the best job she can for her customers. Rachel's house cleaning business on the other hand has the same primary concern, but has also taken it upon herself to understand what other services a homeowner might use on a regular basis. Rachel asked her clients on her regular semi-annual review of her company to list five other businesses they use for work around the home. What Rachel found was that the most used business categories were pest control, lawn care, home shopping services, landscaping, and pool services. After reviewing the information, Rachel decided that four of the five services she couldn't easily do, but one she could. The next week she brought her teenage daughter Beth who was in need of a job around to her clients and said that Beth would be happy to take her mom's car while she was cleaning and get all the grocery shopping done at the store. Also, since they were already going to be there, she could also offer a price discount. Eventually, Rachel was able to put together her own group of five primary vendors and introduce them all to her current and new customers. These other four also did the same for her, and slowly all five companies' businesses prospered more than they could have imagined by simply understanding what other primary needs their customers had. Mary was stuck having to compete with those potential feeder sources instead of tapping into the growth that comes from business collaboration.

Having these seemingly simple six questions answered for any new entrepreneurial business is one of the major differences between people who truly succeed in a market versus people who barely squeak by in their existence. A business that has all of this information planned out from day one has a focused intensity that creates energy and momentum; every step is a goal, and every goal met is an achievement. People in any industry who have a plan feel like they know what they need to do, and where they are going. They feel proud of their achievements and by meeting their goals they will become more self-confident and successful. This is one of the benefits to being an entrepreneur – the ability to get this kind of feedback on a daily basis without having to try to illicit that information from a traditional boss.

Defining a Business

It is often said that a business is defined by its employees or team members, and that is philosophically correct. However, for a start-up, there are certain operating constraints that have to be put in place for accounting and legal purposes. For example, are you going to be a Corporation or a Limited Liability Corporation or a Sole Proprietorship? Also, are you going to use a Cash Flow Based Accounting Method or an Accrual Based Accounting Method? Because I am neither an accountant nor an attorney, I highly recommend getting a good business attorney and accountant to speak with you about getting started, because each state has differences in how these must be set up and the specific benefits associated with them since they are governed under state law.

When I first began looking for an attorney and accountant I had no idea where to turn because I had never used either of them before. I decided to try to find an accountant first because more people I knew seemed to have recommendations on whom to talk to. I think the first rule of thumb when looking for an accountant is that you have to basically rule out the months of February to May. Most busy accountants have little to no time at this point in the year, and if they do fit you in, they might have other things on their minds distracting them from focusing on you. The best way to begin your search for a good accountant is by asking friends, family, and searching online. You can make an appointment with multiple ones, and really take your time in interviewing them and letting them know your situation and analyzing the solutions they propose. Personally, there were three major components that I judged an accountant on when searching. First was appearance – of both the office and the person. If they seemed unorganized or undisciplined, it probably wasn't the accountant for me. Second was how transparent their billing was. I don't like issuing unlimited lines of credit so I expect nothing to appear on bills that I didn't know about as well as the approximate price. Third and very important for entrepreneurs, I wanted an accountant who was like me and entrepreneurial. These types of people are more likely to teach you about business as you go along and make you aware of business pitfalls in addition to accounting ones. Most importantly, make sure you are comfortable with the people actually doing the work on your business and not just the person explaining the product offerings. It is not uncommon for you to meet with a partner of the firm or a business development specialist in the case of large firms. If you like that person and feel comfortable with him or her, it doesn't mean you will feel comfortable with the service provided behind the scene.

The things I looked for in an attorney were similar, but slightly different. A business attorney can help you create your company if you choose to incorporate, but if you are a single member LLC or a sole proprietorship you can accomplish this online yourself. You may wish, however like I did, to consult an attorney in drafting your first contract or engagement letter.

One of the first things I learned when looking for an attorney to help me draft my first contract was that the bigger the firm, the bigger the cost. That's not to say that I haven't met solo attorneys who were expensive – I have, but it's practically a guarantee that larger firms cater to larger corporations that have larger budgets. I went for the smaller firm.

The thing that differentiates working with an attorney and working with an accountant is time. You want as much time to be used by

Enough Dreaming

yourself researching and coming up with the ideas before you start contacting attorneys because they become expensive quickly. When I began interviewing attorneys I predominately looked to ones that specialized in business law and ones that had been around long enough to not make me their trial run of a contract. I then made our initial consultation as fast as possible and over the phone where I basically let him know that I was starting a new company and I needed a contract that included certain services I provided. I also told him that I had no problem writing up contracts so if he had a similar one already completed which I could work off and modify to fit my needs, I would do the grunt work and he could bill me for the finishing touches. That worked out perfectly, and I acquired my first contract that lasted me for years for $350.

    I feel it is important to talk about a second situation that came about with working with attorneys a few years later. Over time and having networked continuously, I became friends with a few attorneys, and when I wanted to create a new contract that incorporated new services my company had begun providing I thought nothing of working with one of their big firms. Now my contact wasn't in the contract-writing field so he introduced me to the person who was and we sat down to talk. He asked me all about how I knew his co-worker and how I started the company as well as where I worked before. An hour into the meeting we finally started getting into the details of the contract and ran through about five or six hypothetical situations so he could understand how it might need to be worded. I left the big downtown building feeling like I just bought a winning lottery ticket. About four weeks later I received an email from this attorney I met containing a rough draft of my contract which was 24 pages long as well as an invoice for $2800, which included the hour of small talk before we even began talking about my business. I was utterly flabbergasted, but I learned an important lesson that day. Big firms are designed for big clients with big needs and even bigger budgets.

Types of Businesses

All businesses have positives and negatives involved with them. Because of this, it is best to take things slowly and "upgrade" yours to one that's more complex and involved only when you need it or you will be jumping through unnecessary hoops. The three general types of businesses are sole proprietorships, partnerships, and corporations. A very brief overview of these three are as follows:

Sole Proprietorships

Sole proprietorships are the simplest to begin and typically done by simply registering a fictitious name filing within your state and county. If you want to look up the government based state site, you should be able to find your specific one by searching "your state business lookup." For example, in Florida it is sunbiz.org and in Georgia it's under the secretary of state's website at cgov.sos.state.ga.us. If you search online for "corporation listings in [your state]," you should be able to find the government site quickly. In each state there is a directory to see what business names are taken and which names are available, so you should keep this in mind before you fall in love with a name. Once you find a name you will need to simply register a DBA (Doing Business As) in order to create your sole proprietorship if you wish to use a name other than your given name. Once this is complete, you will frequently need to file for a business license or permit through your local county or city for a minimal cost. The local municipality will have you register the type of business and whether you are providing a service to others or selling retail goods through a storefront or online.

There are certain criteria that require a sole proprietorship to file for a federal employer identification number (EIN), and one of them is the decision to hire employees. An easy way to postpone this step is to consider using independent contractors (1099's) instead of W2 employees, which we will cover more in depth in the human resources section of this book. Many things can be accomplished through start-ups as a sole proprietorship, and you can choose to turn it into a partnership or a corporation fairly easily. Some other things you may wish to consider during this step are looking up website domain names and trademark registrations so that you can protect your brand as it grows. Searching for trademarks can be done online at the US Patent and Trademark Office (uspto.gov) and domains can be searched through any of the multiple domain hosting companies (Hostmaster, iPage, 1&1, etc.). We will review online growth strategies more under the Strategic Management section.

Partnerships

Partnerships are typically one step removed from a sole proprietorship. A partnership occurs when there is ownership and profit sharing between two or more people. There are various types of partnerships, some of them not available in all states. A general partnership is basic, where two or more people are partners, share profits, and are personally linked to the company for any liability. Because so few people like that personal liability, limited liability and limited partnerships have been created as well as combinations of the two. In partnerships, the business takes on a more complicated form where each partner is issued or buys a certain percentage of ownership of the business and is then issued that amount of the profits when distributed. General partnerships do not typically provide any sort of legal protection to the owners and are merely a contractual way of dividing up the profits in an equitable manner based on their job duties. The major benefit of creating a partnership over a corporation is that the reporting requirement is relatively low and the business operates more like a sole proprietorship. I am not a fan of partnerships personally due to the fact that it doesn't offer much more liability protection than a sole proprietorship except for limited liability partnerships which act more like corporations. If you wish to offer an employee some profit sharing to keep them incentivized and engaged, you could do so without giving up actual ownership of the company, and you remain a sole proprietorship. Just be prepared to open your accounting books to the employee getting a share of the profits or they may feel like they are being deceived. All state, county, and federal registration remains the same for partnerships, as do the trademarking and domain registration processes.

Corporations

Businesses that have multiple employees and offer a variety of benefits frequently form corporations. What separates corporations from the rest of the options is the legal protection it offers owners' personal assets. If you are the owner and not doing a lot of the liability-based activities to produce your product, you may want to consider a corporation for the protection it offers. What this means is that if your position as the owner involves running the day to day operations, overseeing marketing strategy, and taking care of payroll and bookkeeping, you should incorporate. However, if you are involved in the sales process or are still physically doing the service or creating the product at least partially yourself, if the company were to get sued you would be as liable as a company entity.

There are many types of corporations including Limited Liability Corporations (LLC's), Type S Corporations (or small business corporations), and Type C Corporations. LLC's have displaced many partnerships because they function very similarly to a partnership but also allow for some personal liability protection. LLC's, like partnerships, issue ownership through percentage of the company. Type S Corporations are in between LLC's and Type C Corporations in how they function. These tend to take on more of an entity in themselves but still pass through the profits to the owners to be

Enough Dreaming

reported on the individual tax returns. These differ distinctly from LLC's, however, in how ownership is issued. S Corp's issue stock to the owners and that stock can be sold to other employees or sold to outside investors. Stock differs from straight ownership percentage since the company can also issue new stock in order to bring on new owners. Type C Corporations are by far the most complicated business to operate because they exist as an entity unto itself. This type of business gets taxed based on its own tax rate, and profits can be distributed amongst the owners based on shareholder positions through stock purchases. These distributions of C Corp profits are also taxed on the owners' individual income tax statements in the form of capital gains, whereas in the case of S Corp's, the distributions are only taxed once in the form of ordinary earned income.

Keep in mind that the more complicated the business you create, the more the costs associated with running the company will be - from both the accounting and legal standpoint (from managing your books and doing your taxes to drafting agreements and contracts). As I mentioned before and will reiterate, these corporations are created and maintained on the state level, so it is imperative that you have a good accountant and legal advisor involved in the creation and maintenance of your business.

When considering which business entity is best for you in your situation, you should also consider consulting with an insurance agent. There are many products available to business owners that act as an isolation for litigation against your personal assets. Some types of insurance to look into are general liability insurance, business owner's policies (BOP), professional liability insurance, and director's and officer's insurance. You should weigh the costs and protections these offer against different incorporation options, and the solution may be a blend of both options.

What you are looking for as you interview agents is someone who is more interested in teaching you about what insurance products are available, what they can do for your business, and why you

Defining a Business

\multicolumn{6}{c}{***BUSINESS ENTITIES BROKEN DOWN***}
Type	Start-Up Cost	Personal Asset Protection	Ownership Defined By	Liability Protection Costs	Accounting and Legal Costs
Sole Prop.	$	None	Percentage	$$$	$
Partnership	$	None	Percentage	$$$	$$
LLC	$	Yes, Not Directly Involved	Percentage	$$	$$
S-Corp	$$	Yes, Not Directly Involved	Shares	$$	$$$
C-Corp	$$$	Yes	Shares	$	$$$$$

should consider them, rather than someone who is just interested in "pushing product" and selling you policies that provide him or her the best commissions. In this space, like most of the business associates you work with, you need to get multiple opinions. And always ask two questions of them:

1) Do you frequently work with small businesses like mine?

2) Can you provide me with references (names of other clients you work with in similar situations to mine and their contact information for me to talk to them)?

Frequently sales agents will say that they have done similar projects countless times, but they won't be able to actually produce any

Enough Dreaming

proof that they have. Working with an insurance agent that uses your business as a testing ground to try a theory they have learned can end up being costly to your organization in the long run.

Remember that as an entrepreneur you have to put together your team of advisors to create the best structure for your business for long-term viability. Screen thoroughly and work with a good accountant, lawyer, and insurance agent to have the best possible outcomes.

NECESSARY ADVISORY TEAM

```
        Accountant
         ↙     ↘
     Lawyer ⇄ Insurance Agent
```

Operational Management

When many entrepreneurs think about operations management, they immediately picture someone focusing on throughput analysis for a company or perhaps some other product-based management connotation. The reality for start-ups is that there can be a lot of management needed that doesn't revolve around actually producing your product or service or involve selling it. All of these components make up this operational management section.

Operations management is frequently the most daunting aspect of starting a new business for entrepreneurs. Luckily, many small start-ups won't have to worry about this at first, but it is still a good idea to have a plan for when these milestones occur. From a basic accounting section to human resources, banking, real estate, and retirement, this chapter will give you the overview needed to succeed. The main things to keep in mind while reading this is that if you put together your team of advisors, you can lean on them for support in asking these kinds of questions when the situation arises.

Accounting

Even though I have taken accounting courses in my undergraduate degree program and in my master's degree program, it is fair to say that accounting is my least favorite subject. The good thing about the modern day practice of accounting is that current

Enough Dreaming

software such as QuickBooks lets anyone perform accounting fairly easily and there are always professionals to ask when you run into a problem. While we could get into a lot of the minutia here in this section, I want to focus on the most practical accounting advice I can provide that some certified public accountants (CPA's) may not focus on themselves.

Accounting for small businesses consists of two major components – the first is considered tax accounting and the second is what we'll call managerial accounting. Tax accounting revolves around tax season and typically consists of both personal and business tax preparation from February through April 15th of every year. I am a firm believer that using a good CPA for this function is well worth the money. For starters, the services they provide are tax deductible so you are able to recover some of the cost, but more importantly the tax code changes so frequently that if you aren't eating and breathing in that world you will probably misfile something or not get all the deductions you are entitled to. People who file their own taxes instead of using a CPA firm are more frequently audited due to these common discrepancies.

A good CPA will explain how they filed your personal and business taxes and what you can do you improve your deductions by comparing your standard deductions to an itemized deduction statement. For example, increasing your charitable giving, or even outsourcing your major printing jobs can lower your taxable income. Currently, charitable giving and paying a print company for materials are both 100% tax deductible. What this means for your personal taxes is that if you give $10,000 to a qualified 501c3 charitable organization you will be able to get back your ordinary income tax rate from this in a tax refund or in less money you owe at the end of the year. So if your personal tax rate at your highest qualifying bracket is 25%, you will receive back or deduct $2500 from your taxes. Within businesses, spending $10,000 in print services

Operations Management

will count as a $10,000 write off from the cash you received, so you won't end up being taxed on any of the money at all.

Now back to our example. If instead of paying a print company to do your flyers for $10,000, you decided to buy ink and paper and do it yourself, you would only be able to deduct 50% of those expenses on your taxes, and you would count the other $5,000 as profit that you have to pay taxes on – even if you don't have $5,000 because you spent it all on print supplies. This is an important category to be aware of so you don't print unnecessary items that can be outsourced to another company for a write-off.

There are other categories that offer only a 50% write-off as well or have restrictions, so be very diligent about minimizing them. Some common ones are Meals and Entertainment as well as Travel Expenses. If you take a business associate out to a dinner you paid for, you can only deduct 50% of that meal because according to the IRS, you are deducting your guest's meal but yours is a personal expense that is not deductible. By knowing this about meals and entertainment expenses, the next time you bring a group of people out you can consider paying for yours separately. By doing this you personally pay for your $50, but fully write off the other $500 as promotional gift. Otherwise you would be left with a $275 tax liability.

For travel expenses the rule of thought is that if you take a trip for business it has to be exclusively appropriate. So, for example, if you took a trip to Denver for a weekend conference and took your wife with you because you were going to spend the week, there are limits on the deductions. Your flight is deductible but her flight wouldn't be. The hotel room for the days of the conference would be deductible but the days following would not. If you chose to drive, however, you can expense the cost of gas no matter if you bring yourself or your whole family since you'd be paying the same amount in gas regardless of the occupants in the vehicle. By sticking as closely as possible to fully deductible categories, you will be able to make your bank account balance as close to your taxable income for the business as possible come year end.

Frequently, CPA's who do your taxes offer managerial accounting packages for small businesses that are fairly inexpensive. Some even require one of these packages to be purchased in tandem with tax preparation since the information they require at the end of the year is dependent on your managerial accounting duties. These duties include bookkeeping and payroll. It is important that you keep up with these things frequently and that you do so in a completely separate manner from your personal accounts. I had an experience where a bookkeeper had mistyped the year-end balance from my bank account, and nearly cost me thousands of dollars so it is very important if you outsource this function to still be very vigilant in your understanding of the statements and reports.

When you come from the world of working for someone else, all you have to worry about with taxes is filing before April 15th. When you own a business, however, you have to pay the government throughout the year in estimated quarterly earnings statements or, at a minimum, set aside the money that you may need and don't touch it unless you want to owe a lot of money at the end of the year. One of the biggest mistakes that new businesses make is to not allocate enough money for their end of the year taxes. When you have just started your dream business and are all excited to make something of it, once you receive that first check the last thing on your mind is setting some of it aside for taxes. You are interested in buying new supplies, upgrading your equipment, hiring help, and putting literal food on your table – not paying the tax man. Unfortunately, the tax man requires his pound of flesh, so to speak, so you should make sure you create a system that keeps you from spending "his" money.

Once you begin your business, you should open up a business checking account with a bank. All business income should be deposited into this account so that you pay all business related expenses from this account. When you cut payroll checks to yourself or to employees, you should have yet another account considered an escrow account for paying your quarterly taxes. A payroll service will do this automatically for you so you aren't misled into thinking you have more money available than you actually do and then end up owing the IRS a lot of money at the end of the year with some assessed penalties.

Another idiosyncrasy of owning your own business when it comes to taxes is the additional tax burden the business has. You personally may end up being in the 25% tax bracket at the end of the year, but you have to remember that the government also taxes your business separately. Medicare and social security both basically double for businesses so you have to pay approximately 7.65% personally and then your business has to match it owing an additional 7.65%. So when you are setting aside money for your quarterly tax burden, be sure to add in an additional 10% to be safe. For example, if you calculate your personal taxes at 25%, you should set aside around a third of the money you withdraw for personal income to take into consideration your total tax burden.

One massage therapist I knew opened up her own massage business on the side of the company she was working for. Throughout the year, she was about to make an additional $40,000 by setting up a little studio in her house and having clients come to her house during times her day job wasn't open. At the end of the year she figured she would just pay her taxes out of next years' profits instead of setting money aside. Unfortunately, her total income for the year was $75,000 which put her in a completely different tax bracket than her $35,000 work income – plus she has to pay self-employment social security and Medicare on top of her regular federal income taxes. Instead of paying 13%, she now had to pay 26% of the extra $40,000 and owed the IRS what turned out to be over $10,000. If she has just set aside 25% to 33% into a tax escrow account throughout

Enough Dreaming

the year as she earned it, she would have just about all the money needed already set aside when she was filing her taxes.

2015 Tax Tables - Individual Taxpayers

If Taxable Income is:	Plus Business Tax:	The Tax Due Is:
0-$9,225	7.65%	17.65% of taxable income
$9,226 -$37,450	7.65%	$1,628.21 + 22.65% of the amount over $9,225
$37,451 -$90,750	7.65%	$8,020.92 + 32.65% of the amount over $37,450
$90,751 -$189,300	7.65%	$25,423.04 + 35.65% of the amount over $90,750
$189,301 -$411,500	7.65%	$60,555.76 + 40.65% of the amount over $189,300
$411,501 -$413,200	7.65%	$150,879.65 + 42.65% of the amount over $411,500
$413,201+	7.65%	$151,604.27 + 47.25% of the amount over $413,200

Example

If you earned $115,000 as a single entrepreneur in your own business you would owe:

$25,423.04 + ($115,000-$90,750) x 35.65%

= $25,423.04 + $8,645.13

= $34,068.17

This would put you in a realized tax bracket of 30% at the end of the year.

Enough Dreaming

2015 Tax Tables - Married Individuals Filing Joint Tax Returns & Surviving Spouses

If Taxable Income is Between:	Plus Business Tax:	The Tax Due Is:
0-$18,450	7.65%	17.65% of taxable income
$18,451 -$74,900	7.65%	$3,256.42 + 22.65% of the amount over $18,450
$74,901 -$151,200	7.65%	$16,040.12 + 32.65% of the amount over $74,900
$151,201 -$230,450	7.65%	39,951.74 + 35.65% of the amount over $151,200
$230,451 -$411,500	7.65%	$68,204.01 + 40.65% of the amount over $230,450
$411,501 -$464,850	7.65%	$141,800.43 + 42.65% of the amount over $411,500
$464,850+	7.65%	$163,553.78 + 47.25% of the amount over $464,850

Example

If you earned $115,000 as a married entrepreneur filing jointly in your own business you would owe:

$16,040.12 + ($115,000-$74,900) x 32.65%

= $16,040.12 + $13,092.65

= $29,132.77

This would put you in a realized tax bracket of 25% at the end of the year.

2015 Tax Tables - Married Individuals Filing Separate Tax Returns

If Taxable Income is Between:	Plus Business Tax:	The Tax Due Is:
0-$9,225	7.65%	17.65% of taxable income
$9,226 -$37,450	7.65%	$1,628.21 + 22.65% of the amount over $9,225
$37,451 -$75,600	7.65%	$8,020.95 + 32.65% of the amount over $37,450
$75,601 -$115,225	7.65%	$20,476.60 + 35.65% of the amount over $76,600
$115,226 -$205,750	7.65%	$34,602.56 + 40.65% of the amount over $115,225
$205,751 -$232,425	7.65%	$71,400.56 + 42.65% of the amount over $205,750
$232,426+	7.65%	$82,777.02 + 47.25% of the amount over $232,426

Example

If you earned $115,000 as a married entrepreneur filing separately in your own business you would owe:

$20,476.60 + ($115,000-$75,601) x 35.65%

= $14,045.74 + $20,476.60

= $34,522.34

This would put you in a realized tax bracket of 30% at the end of the year.

Enough Dreaming

Bookkeeping

While bookkeeping isn't necessarily the most enjoyable activity for most entrepreneurs, it is essential for the management of the organization. Bookkeeping is simply the categorization of the spending and income of a business, so that you know where the money is going and where it is coming from. Once you have this information processed, it provides a whole world of information that can answer questions such as:

How much does it cost for me on average to acquire a customer?

Should I keep this customer or are they costing me more than I make on them?

How much is my business worth?

Am I putting too much money into any one area of my business?

How much are my profit margins, given the cost of producing my product?

By keeping up with your bookkeeping, you will not only be able to answer questions your accountant will have for tax preparation, but you will also have a financial grasp of the operations of your company. That knowledge will allow you to allocate money to the right areas of your business while limiting the funds being placed in areas that are not as fruitful.

In order to begin bookkeeping, there are three different options to consider for most start-ups. The first option is to hire someone to do this for you – either a branch of an accounting firm, an employee within your company, or an independent bookkeeping company. Hiring someone can cost as little at $150 per month to $300-$400 per month depending on whom you hire and how much time they need to put into this, as well as how much you are going to do on

Operations Management

your end. Therefore, this option is typically best for people who have a good amount of business from day one and value their time being freed up most of all because they have too much to do. Unless you started your business by taking your existing job and turning it into an entrepreneurial venture, you probably won't have enough work to justify this expense at first.

The second bookkeeping option for entrepreneurs beginning bookkeeping is to purchase a program to assist you with the proper categorization and organization such as QuickBooks. This software can typically cost a few hundred dollars and may have a monthly cost for support if you need it. This is the best option for many entrepreneurs because it not only forces you to know your own business's information, but it also fills a need for all the entrepreneurs with control issues (which are a lot of them). This cost is typically only beneficial if you are planning on continuing to do your bookkeeping into the future. If you start doing your own bookkeeping, just to decide a month later that you can't keep up with it and you will pay a company instead, it was money wasted. Sometimes a solution for that is doing a 30 day trial of the program, which is typically free, so that you can be certain this is the path you would like to take.

The third option for bookkeeping is choosing to do your own the old-fashioned way. Before the software was developed, people used to do bookkeeping with paper ledgers and T Accounts that showed what category money was placed in. While it can seem archaic to people today, this is a very viable and nearly free solution for basic entrepreneurs. And if the idea of paper doesn't appeal to you, you can also create spreadsheets that do the same thing on your computer or tablet. If you start a side business and you are still figuring out how to get new clients, you can learn how to record the one sale you did the first month this way to keep your costs down while learning the basic principles of accounting. Once you get things going in your business you can always switch over to a program or hire someone to do it; however, there is no need to rush into anything at the beginning.

Three Bookkeeping Options for Entrepreneurs

Spreadsheets → Software → Outsource

Financial Statements

There are four major financial statements that you should be familiar with as a business owner: Balance Sheets, Income Statements, Statement of Cash Flows, and Statement of Retained Earnings. These are all statements that a CPA or trained bookkeeper can review with you; however, this section will give a brief overview of them.

Balance Sheets

Balance sheets are a review of your business's assets and liabilities. A liability is a debt outstanding or yet to be paid. An asset is anything of value that the company owns including cash on hand, equipment, land or buildings, vehicles, outstanding bills owed to you (known as accounts receivables), outstanding loans provided (known as notes receivables), and prepaid bills. Prepaid bills would be things such as insurance or cell phone plans, where if you were to cancel the policy you would receive cash back or a deposit on hold with the company. Liabilities are the opposite of assets and consist of debts outstanding, which may include wages owed to employees, taxes owed to the government, or interest owed on rental equipment. What is left over, once you subtract your liabilities from your assets, is called owner's equity or retained earnings. This sheet essentially shows how much money would be leftover if you were to liquidate your company at a given time.

$$\frac{\begin{array}{c}\textit{Assets }(\textit{What you Own})\\ -\textit{ Liabilities }(\textit{What you Owe})\end{array}}{=\textit{Owner's Equity }(\textit{Value in Company})}$$

Income Statements

Income statements are also known as profit and loss statements or P&L statements. These statements give a quick glance of revenue coming in and debts paid for a period of time whether that is quarterly, semi-yearly, or yearly. There are many ways that businesses choose to look at this statement that an accountant can review further with you. Some of these views include: EBIT (Earnings Before Interest and Taxes) or EBITA (Earnings Before Interest, Taxes and Amortization). If your business has a lot of equipment to depreciate, you may want to look at the actual profits before write offs; however, if that is not the case, you may be more interested in the bottom line profit that includes amortization since that isn't a large line item for your business. This statement is extremely important to familiarize yourself with so you can keep an eye on your expenses and try to limit unnecessary ones as you grow, while maximizing the most profitable areas.

$$\frac{\begin{array}{c}\textit{Income}\\ -\textit{ Debts Paid}\end{array}}{=\textit{Earnings }(\textit{Before Deductions, Taxes and Upcoming Payments Due})}$$

Statement of Cash Flows

When you think of the statement of cash flows, consider picturing a river of cash. As income comes into the company, it spreads like a river, and where it goes shows how it is being spent. What is left over on the statement of cash flows is your cash position which is how much money you essentially have in the bank at any given time. This is one of the most familiar statements for most business owners because personal bank statements come in this fashion and simply provide an overview of what cash came in, where it was allocated, and how much cash is currently in the bank, for a snapshot in time.

Statement of Retained Earnings

Statements of retained earnings show how much equity is in the company from the balance sheet and what was done with these earnings. Your retained earnings are calculated by taking your beginning equity position for the period, adding in investments and income, and subtracting any withdrawals from owner's equity. The easiest way to think about retained earnings is that it represents how much of a savings account the business has built within the company.

Suppose at the end of five consecutive years a company had $100,000 in operating profits which are then taxed. $100,000 in profit in this example would require a tax liability of $30,000 so the owner decides to take out $50,000 of that $100,000 so the taxes can be covered. That would leave $50,000 of profit now rolled into the "owner's equity" category because the taxes on it have already been "prepaid" even though the whole $100,000 was not technically withdrawn from the company. After five years of this, the company would have $250,000 of owner's equity, but that doesn't mean the company has $250,000 in an account just waiting to be withdrawn. You would have to look at all the financial statements to get an idea of the true state of the company. Because of situations like this, I truly stress the importance of having a good, competent CPA in your corner, because even trained business professionals such as myself sometimes find my head spinning after looking at financial statements.

$$\frac{\begin{array}{l}\textit{Equity}\\ +\textit{ Investments and Income}\\ -\textit{ Withdrawals}\end{array}}{=\textit{Retained Earnings or Owner's Equity}}$$

All of these statements are important for business owners to understand in order to maximize the efforts of their operation. Luckily, you will only need a basic understanding to start and grow a business and will only need to dig deeper into their meanings once your main challenge is no longer gaining new customers.

Human Resources

Hiring, firing and managing employees can be one of the most challenging aspects of running a business. I am a firm believer that if you don't have to employ someone, and can legally contract with them for their services, it will save you a lot of headaches during your growth phase. Many human resource professionals have demeanors like attorneys because what they have to know is entrenched in legalities and technicalities. So as you consider venturing into this arena do so with as much knowledge as possible.

There are many HR resources online for new businesses, such as the Small Business Administration, that can help give guidance on ways to approach hiring and firing and the appropriate path to take when doing so. If you are extremely determined to know more about this business segment, you should consider familiarizing yourself with some federal and state compliance guidelines such as the IRS guidelines on appropriately classifying workers, the Department of Labor's Fair Labor Standards Act (FLSA), and the Federal Equal Employment Opportunity (EEO) Laws.

The reason I believe in starting a business by bringing on independent contractors rather than employees is that it saves you a lot of headaches in dealing with people. By contracting with an independent contractor, you are basing work on a contract with defined duties and goals rather than an open ended promise to pay regardless of the work done, which is what you get with employment contracts. Let's begin by considering what makes up an independent contractor versus an employee in the eyes of the IRS.

Appropriate Classification of Workers

There are two basic classifications of workers – a W2 employee or a 1099 independent contractor. A CPA is a great resource for this, as they can advise you on which is more appropriate for the situation. For accounting purposes, the difference between these two worker classifications is that W2's are under the business umbrella and you have to pay additional employer taxes on top of withholding and submitting their federal, state, and city taxes on their behalf. There are other considerations that having W2's bring such as liabilities, worker's compensation insurance, and state unemployment tax, but for this purpose we will focus on the accounting basics. 1099's function essentially as vendors to your business, and you have to simply write a check to them. They are responsible for setting aside taxes and filing everything on their own, independently.

When put like that, you might wonder why you wouldn't want everyone to be a 1099 instead of a W2, but there are certain job constraints that define which bucket is most appropriate for their individual duties. The IRS gives general guidelines that help determine whether a worker is a W2 or a 1099. W2's do not have the right to control their own actions and can be told how to do their job. 1099's are typically given a contract for a lump sum payment for certain products or end results. W2's are compensated in a way that keeps their time and expenses in mind. That may include reimbursement for expenses by the business, but they are provided all the tools they need to complete their duties such as a business computer or vehicle. 1099's are expected to own their own equipment and to manage their expenses within the agreed upon allotment.

Lastly, what kind of relationship does the business have with the worker? Are there benefits provided such as insurance, sick time, or vacation time? Those are W2 benefits and not something a 1099 would receive. Also is there an expectation of work to be performed for the relationship to continue? If you are given a task as a W2 and you fall behind or fail at completing the task, it doesn't necessarily result in the discontinuation of your services; whereas if a 1099 doesn't complete the tasks given, it is assumed that no more work will be offered.

The appropriate classification of employees is an area of the law that is taken advantage of by many businesses. If you are caught miscategorizing a W2 as a 1099, however, your business can be held responsible for paying the entire employer taxes due that have not been correctly paid and the fees associated with late payments. If you have a worker and are unclear which status to put them in, you can file a form SS-8 with the IRS and they will let you know which status is most appropriate for them.

To give a practical example of this, we can go back to our lawn care business. If you gain enough work that you need someone to help and they are expected to ride with you and use your equipment to complete a job, they should be classified as W2 employees. If you want to add on more customers and just don't have the time, you might consider hiring a 1099 contractor to service those extra lawns for you, and they would complete the job independently over the course of a predetermined set time. You could even rent them your equipment to use in the contract agreement, if you wanted to get

Enough Dreaming

creative, but they would have to provide their own insurance, gas, and anything else needed to complete the job.

Two major distinctions between a W2 and a 1099 for your business security is the issue of non-competes and outside work. W2 employees can and are frequently upheld to non-competes and non-disclosure agreements where your customer base and trade secrets are safe. 1099 independent contractors have much less constraints on them, and are free to work for your competitors in conjunction with working with your business, unless stated specifically in your contract. Secondly, 1099's are often defined by their having multiple clients and contracts for their income source and are free to do so. If you have a 1099 whose sole client is your business it lends itself to a W2 classification. So, in the example above of a 1099 that rents your equipment to mow lawns, it would be within their right to use that same equipment to mow other lawns and make a profit for themselves directly or for a competing lawn service.

Fair Labor Standards

The Fair Labor Standards Act (FLSA) takes the IRS guidelines on worker status and multiplies the complexity by 100, once they are determined to be a W2 employee. Now you have to consider whether the position is classified as exempt (a salaried employee) or non-exempt (an hourly employee). FLSA includes such things as minimum wage levels, reimbursement guidelines, required break periods, minimum age requirement, worker's compensation insurance, employee classification exemptions, etc. This area is very complex and can be overwhelming for entrepreneurs who just want to build a company and not have to deal with this minutia. The best way to approach it is to familiarize yourself with the act or hire a HR company to do a positional review of your company to make sure people are classified correctly and treated fairly. Another crucial piece of managing this aspect of a business is having an employee handbook. An employee handbook is a detailed organizational overview on business policies. A human resources company could easily customize one of their state specific templates to your organization, and this would also give you a good playbook to understand how you need to treat your employees. Having this document, and having employees sign off on reading and understanding it after hiring them, is a good way to protect your business from miscommunication at best and employee lawsuits at worst. Definitely seek advice from a qualified human resources company or labor law attorney when you begin down this path.

Hiring

Federal Equal Employment Opportunity (EEO) laws cover all sorts of anti-discrimination issues revolving around hiring, retaining, compensation, testing, promotions, recruiting, and firing employees. This, like the other areas of employment law, should be reviewed with a qualified HR company or labor law attorney if you want to make sure you are dotting all your "i's" and crossing all your "t's" correctly.

Because this area of starting a business is so complicated, I will leave you with the takeaways that I had from dealing with this. For starters, not every EEO law will pertain to your business, but you should act as if they do from day one so you don't have to worry about modifying your policies as your company grows from 19 to 20 employees, for example. Secondly, the best employees are recruited and not hired. If you post a job online you can spend hundreds to thousands of dollars running ads to fill your open positions. What if, instead, you were to go up to the extremely personable and likable individual that you happen to meet at a store and who makes an impression on you and let them know your situation, that you like their energy and attitude, and if they'd like to have a second interview you would love to discuss your needs and their talents more, since the first informal interview you just had impressed you.

Enough Dreaming

This is why so many large companies provide hiring bonuses to employees who recommend the job to others who join.

If you do decide to hire by way of job posting and traditional interviews, you will see very quickly how overwhelming the number of applicants you can get and how frustrating the process can be. The first time I posted a job was for an administrative assistant. That help wanted ad online ended up costing me about $500, and I received nearly 1600 applicants since it was right in the middle of a recession. There was no way for me at the time to know how to reduce the number so I just started interviewing. I found that half the people didn't show up to their interviews, and of the half that did, maybe 25% were qualified to do the job. What I did from there was try and work backward to determine what qualities made up the 25% who were reasonable applicants.

Some of the things that I had to look at in order to tap into the right candidates for the position were:

Did they complete the application fully?

Are there any major gaps in time in their resume?

Do they have a cover letter?

Did they send a thank you card (post interview process)?

Did they write to confirm their interview appointment?

Are they actually qualified?

Do they live close by?

By using these criteria for consideration, it allowed me to not only narrow down the applicants to a manageable number but it also weeded out people who were mailing their resume to anyone and everyone, as well as people who didn't really want a job but wanted proof on paper that they are looking in order to keep unemployment benefits or financial benefits.

Operations Management

Total Applicants for Position: 15,705

Completed Job Application Form: 3,549

Salary Requirement within Range: 2,988

No Gaps in Time on Resume: 1,957

Cover Letter Included: 251

Live Within 30 Minutes: 62

In this example, assuming an average of 15 minutes allocated for first interviews, you just cut your potential interview time from nearly 4000 hours to 15.5 hours. Some people may ask if there's a possibility of eliminating good qualified candidates this way, and my response would be a resounding absolutely! But your goal as a small business owner is to weigh the time needed to find your perfect employee with the amount of time it takes to sift through their competition. If you can find a good, but possibly great, employee with 15.5 hours of time vs. a great employee after taking possibly over two years of dedicated time where I generate no money, then a good employee it is. Besides, most of the time they aren't just good, but great because they have already shown the quality traits you need. They are thorough, asking for a reasonable salary, truthful, detail oriented, and prompt. Once you have more revenue and you have other people to whom you can delegate the first round of interviews, I'd say interviewing more applicants doesn't pose as much of an opportunity cost. (An opportunity cost is the difference between the total amount of time and effort needed for one outcome versus another outcome.)

Another consideration when hiring employees is the use of background searches, credit checks, and hiring for character and cultural fits to your organization. Background searches in the past used to mean just checking someone's criminal history, but today it is also includes checking someone's social media profiles. By checking someone's social media pages such as Facebook, Twitter, Instagram, LinkedIn, and simply searching their name online, you can often find out more personal aspects about a person that they are necessarily willing to share during an interview, or answers to questions that you cannot legally ask them. Does the person have pictures of them partying and drinking during spring break and then posts about how they flunked a test the next day because of it? Or perhaps it highlights that the person is a single mother who seems to have a hard time getting babysitting coverage? Or lastly, maybe it shows a high level of professionalism where the person highlights photos of their volunteer work at a local shelter or visiting their grandparents in the nursing home. Social media can be a powerful tool to gain further insights into your work candidates that can reveal both negative and positive traits.

Criminal background checks are also a valuable tool when considering someone for employment. You can ask this question legally on employment applications, but many people who have records aren't going to be forthright about their past in these situations. An important point to note about people with criminal records is that you need to determine whether their indiscretion will directly impact the job you are hiring for. If the person has a history of aggressive driving or drunk driving but the job doesn't require any driving, then it should not necessarily be a deal breaker. In the same manner, if the charge against them was petty theft but they aren't going to be working with money, will that really impact their ability to function in their job? The charge's relation to the job itself, in addition to the length of time that has passed since the occurrence, are two things that need to be factored in to a limiting criteria such as background checks. But you shouldn't rule out people with criminal backgrounds that don't impact the job directly. By hiring people with criminal records you can sometimes get a very loyal and dedicated employee out of the deal.

The last kind of check that has emerged in popularity is that of credit checks. The thought behind it is that if the person can maintain good credit, they have a more stable life. This too needs to be weighed quite heavily when limiting a candidate for this reason. Someone might have a good reason for why they have poor credit, and you can simply ask them the story around it instead of immediately limiting them from the pool of approved applicants. However, if you see someone who filed bankruptcy in the last few years, you would think that some poor decisions were made in their lives. The true question is whether they made corrections in their lives since then.

What I have found in running businesses is that hiring can be a tricky part of operations. However, there are some general guidelines I found helpful. First, I never post a job for critical positions because it is too hard to screen people enough to know if they will succeed. And unless I have someone already performing the job, I consider most positions critical positions because they represent myself, my business, and their co-workers every day in the community. Every time I leave the office I'm on a secondary recruiting mission. If I meet someone who treated me well in our doings – getting coffee, checking me out at the grocery store, etc., I am going to try to keep in touch with them because I know they are a "keeper".

Now when I say that I don't advertise for positions, that's just in the beginning stages of developing the business. Once your business expands you will begin to shift from a focus on uncovering business opportunities, to finding the time to meet the demand you currently have. In that situation, I would definitely be a more active ad placer. The tricky part tends to be knowing when that transition happens so you don't find yourself so busy that you have no time to interview. However, this requires balance, because hiring

Enough Dreaming

too quickly will leave you with an employee sitting around doing nothing.

Secondly, I have discovered another critical fact – that it is better to hire someone who needs training in a job's function but has the right fit for your company than hiring someone who has stellar job skills but won't conform to your company culture. What we frequently do in order to determine this is have the applicants take some personality and skills tests to see what their results are. Strengthsfinder2.0 is a book which includes an online test that provides insights into what character strengths someone has. Also the DiSC personality assessment is both an online and paper test that gives a personality overview of the person. Paying money to have people take these two assessments before hiring them is well worth it in determining if they are going to be a good fit for your organization.

Last, there is a saying that I find to be very true, "You can't teach someone how to be hungry." This of course doesn't mean physically hungry, but instead mentally and emotionally hungry. There is a major difference between someone who is hungry versus someone who is just plain greedy. Someone who is mentally hungry has a desire to grow and achieve, and they aren't just looking for a job but for a work outlet to exercise this achievement desire. I believe this is known as someone who is "achievement oriented". If you can get someone who is hungry and looking to make their mark in the world, you have found someone who will really take your business to the next level.

Firing

Before I begin discussing firing employees, I should state again that I am not an attorney and especially not an employment attorney, so if you have questions about your particular situation you should consult with an attorney in your state regarding the particular language within the state laws.

There are different laws for each state, and these laws can be best differentiated by whether it is an at-will state, right to work state, or one that doesn't have those provisions. At-will states refer to the employees being "at will" employees. This gives the majority of the protections to the employer (versus an employee) when it comes to firing. Oppositely, right to work states take the stance that employees have rights as far as the security of their job, and employers will have to provide a long history of documented reasons before they can fire an employee without paying a penalty of sorts. Here are some of the differences that employers can face in different scenarios:

Action 1: At-Will State resided employer fires employee due to loss of revenue

Result: Employee would be qualified to file for state unemployment but would only be paid through the date the employee actually worked, unless stipulated otherwise by employer.

Action 2: Right-to-Work State resided employer fires employee due to loss of revenue

Result: Employee would be qualified to file for state unemployment and would also be qualified to receive addition benefits from employer for terminating without cause.

Action 3: At-Will State resided employer fires employee due to theft of corporate property

Result: Employee would be paid through the contracted final employment date, and if they filed for state unemployment they would only get it if the state representative didn't believe the business had enough proof or did not sufficiently attempt to work with the employee and put him or her on probation.

Enough Dreaming

Action 4: <u>Right-to-Work State resided employer fires employee due to theft of corporate property</u>

Result: Employee would be paid through the contract final employment date, and they would receive state unemployment. If the business did not document their attempts to resolve the issue with the employee by putting them in counseling, trying them at a less stressful job, and providing them with a salary analysis to be certain that this employee wasn't underpaid as the root cause of the theft – then they may have to pay the employee additionally after termination to assist them in finding a comparable job in the future.

Some of these examples may have been a little exaggerated, but the spirit of them is accurate. In At-Will States the burden is on the employee to do their job, and the employer can fire them at any time for any reason. In Right-to-Work States the burden is on the employer to provide the employee with every feasible way to keep them employed. In my mind I picture employees in Right-to-Work States as tenured teachers while At-Will States employ everyone else. It seems to me that a person's productivity and energy that they bring to the workplace should be what keeps their job for them instead of an employer's fear of having to be financially penalized for replacing them.

One more thing that I would like to mention regarding firing employees is the impact on your unemployment taxes. Every company has a multiple that the state assigns, and for every dollar you issue in wages to your employees and yourself, the state takes a percentage of that money and puts it in an escrow account of sorts that they have for your company. When employees are fired and file for unemployment, if they get it and are being paid by the state government, they are actually being paid from an escrow account that you are funding through every employment check that you write. I know the first time that I had to fire an employee and they were awarded unemployment for $400 per week or so, I become quite concerned about this unforeseen cash draw on my business. Luckily, the money to support this had been coming out all along so I didn't have to worry about paying an additional amount. Now there is a negative to having an employee draw unemployment, which is that the more people who are fired and get unemployment, the higher the multiple that the state attaches to you and your employees' wages rises. If you keep turning over employees, you can end up with a much higher multiple and essentially having to pay higher taxes.

The final consideration to make when firing employees is to make sure you have someone in the room to witness the event. I have had unemployment disputes come up where the employee makes claims, about why they were told they were fired, which were not true. If you have a witness to testify as to what happened, it will protect your business from liabilities. In the same way, make sure to have the employee sign a form that explains everything in writing. They can refuse to sign it; however, if you have a witness attest to the fact that they were given the form and had everything on it explained, they will not be able to make facts up.

Banking

Working with banks is an important part of starting any new business. Of course, I mentioned that you have to open a business checking account and use that to manage your business expenses, but there are also other things you need to be aware of when it comes to banking. For starters, I personally believe in having your business and personal accounts in one place if possible. If you do this, you are invested more in one institution and they will be more invested in your success as well. The only downside to this is that if you end up taking out any business loans and default on them, that bank can generally take funds from your personal accounts without a court order in order to repay the debt. One way to work around this concern would be to take out a safety deposit box and put your emergency funds in that instead of directly in an account. With savings rates currently being so low, the amount of interest you give up would be nominal compared to the security of knowing your money is completely safe, since banks cannot seize assets in safety deposit accounts as easily or in the same manner as they can for personal checking or savings accounts.

Another reason I believe in being involved with one bank closely is the benefit that the banking officers can have on your business. Many banks have either a business banker who will be assigned to you, or a bank manager in smaller institutions, whose job is to develop relationships with businesses throughout the community and to make your life easier when interacting with the bank while doing transactions. You can ask a bank before opening an account what kind of business percentages that branch does as compared to personal accounts to get an idea of how heavily they are invested in such business operations. These business bankers or bank managers can be great assets in growing your business. If they understand your business model and can identify good business partners or customers, they will frequently go out of their way to create connections for you within their client base to engender goodwill. These connections, created simply by your being strategic about choosing a good banking partner, can expedite your business's growth.

Secured Loans vs Unsecured Loans

As a general rule, I don't believe in taking out business loans. Instead, you should consider building up your owner's equity in order to invest in new materials or projects when at all possible. However, in the rare case that you cannot cash flow your business investments, here are some pointers that you should be aware of when you are entertaining the idea.

There are two general types of loans – secured and unsecured loans. A secured loan is drawn up with collateral (company assets, buildings, personal assets, etc.) while unsecured loans are created based on a financial history with the business and your personal income. As a start-up, you cannot typically get an unsecured loan or line of credit without having your personal income and accounts taken into consideration, which most banks will only do if you do your personal banking at their institution. If you absolutely have to take out a loan, you should consider only doing secured loans based on your business's assets and not your personal ones. However, by building up your owner's equity in the company, you should be able to bypass having to take out loans altogether, because you will have an ability to use the money from your account without having to concern yourself with the bank's involvement. Keep in mind that you may pay income taxes on the money you use in this way when calculating your tax at the end of the year. When you roll revenue over into owner's equity it is considered income for you, but that's a positive thing. You gain the ability to self-finance as well as increase the value of your business, which we will get to later on.

Real Estate

People in the real estate world are notorious for sayings like "location, location, location" or "visibility equals profitability." What many entrepreneurs don't understand, though, is that you can frequently have a very profitable business by operating out of your house long before you have to consider a visible business location. You should first consider your business plan and think about who your customer is and what their needs are. Many people can transact a sale by meeting the customer at the customer's house, work, or even a public location such as a coffee shop. If that's not your case and you have an actual product that needs to be seen, sampled, or stored, you should consider utilizing the Internet and shipping directly to customers, or using a platform such as eBay or Amazon to get started. Warehousing inventory can be one of the most expensive parts of a retail operation, not to mention that the rent at those locations are among the highest because of the typical visibility involved. What causes many people to jump into getting

Enough Dreaming

a business location is the need to expand your staff, or the prestige involved with having a location.

As far as expanding staffing, there are a variety of options available to businesses through remote or web-based services. For example, if you need a receptionist to answer your calls because you can't get to your phone in a timely manner, you may wish to consider a service that offers a receptionist who will take the calls for you and either transfer the calls, or get messages, to you. You can even provide them with a script to answer basic questions about your business such as your location, pricing, and setting up consultations or follow-up phone calls. If you need an assistant to help do more intensive work than just answering a phone, there are additional options available. You can again work with a remote secretary who will typically teleconference with you during the day allowing you to let them know what needs to be accomplished. This can solve all web-based work that can be shared over the Internet, but you will still have to make your own copies and get your own coffee. If your business is more paper based or you need someone to help physically doing things, check online in your area and you might be surprised to find there are people who don't have the flexibility of working in an office (because they have a child at home, have irregular hours, or care for a sick family member), but are happy to come to you periodically to pick up papers or gather materials and complete the tasks from their house as they are able.

Lastly, as for the prestige that an office provides, there again are many options available to the start-up entrepreneur. For starters, you can purchase an address and list that on your business card to be able to advertise a location that isn't residential. I don't recommend going to the post office for a P.O. Box to accomplish this, but there are plenty of other services that give you an address with a suite number to advertise, and some will even forward your mail to your actual address so you don't have to physically visit their location to get your mail. If this still doesn't solve your dilemma, consider a

Operations Management

suite sharing operation. There are companies that buy a floor of a building and hire a couple of receptionists for multiple businesses at once. That way, you are only paying for a small office and are getting the benefit of having a receptionist, someone to answer phone calls, and access to things such as break rooms, copy machines, or conference rooms for meetings.

Retirement

Many entrepreneurs I come across believe they don't need a retirement account because they believe that their business is their retirement and that they will someday use it to either fund their retirement through the day to day profits or through the sale of the business. This, however, is a fallacy and even entrepreneurs need to concern themselves with funding traditional retirement options. If the business does succeed to produce a profit in the future, that should be considered the icing on the cake and not be depended upon to be the cake itself. There are countless examples of these kinds of things happening, and that's why you see people in their 70's working menial jobs to supplement Medicare and keep the lights on. Perhaps you had a great bakery but suddenly there was a wheat virus that wiped out half the world's crop and tripled your production cost. When you want to sell that business, the buyer won't care that "we used to make a lot more when margins were higher." Or perhaps you owned a car dealership and figured that's a good business because it's backed by a manufacturer – but even manufacturers can and have gone out of business. In the words of Benjamin Franklin, "By failing to prepare, you are preparing to fail."

Entrepreneurs have many options for retirement funding. For starters, there are retirement options available to everyone regardless of employment in the form of Roth Individual Retirement Accounts (Roth IRAs) or Traditional Individual Retirement Accounts (Traditional IRAs). The Roth IRA provides tax-free growth while the Traditional IRA provides tax-deferred growth. To many people, tax-free wins over tax-deferred any day, but I would add the only caveat is when you are presently in a higher tax bracket and are planning on dropping into a lower one. Tax deferring a 40% tax bracket is a lot different than deferring a 15% bracket.

The other consideration between the Traditional IRA and Roth IRA is the income limitations. The Roth had income limitations which ranged between $183,000 to $193,000 for married filing jointly in 2015 and $116,000 to $131,000 for singles. Both the Roth IRAs and the Traditional IRAs have contribution limits each year, currently at $5,500 if you are under 50 years old and $6,500 for "catch up contributions" if you are over 50 years old. One important consideration as a business owner is that unless you are operating a C Corporation, your business profits, whether or not you take them as a salary, are considered income to you at the end of the year. So, if you took a salary of $60,000 but your company shows a profit at the end of the year of $30,000 that you were saving up to buy some equipment, you will show a total income of $90,000 when doing your end of the year taxes. Contributions to retirement accounts will count against income, and will reduce the amount of tax due in the current year.

For retirement plans within a business, entrepreneurs have various options to consider. A Simplified Employee Pension (SEP) IRA allows you to contribute and deduct up to 20 percent of your net self-employment income or 25 percent of your income if you are an employee of your corporation. While the costs to operate a SEP are low, the main consideration is whether you have other employees within your company. If you do, you have to contribute the same percentage of their incomes to their individual retirement. This can be a positive for entrepreneurs who are looking for forward thinking individuals who are okay taking a 25 percent pay cut compared to what they could get at a similar job elsewhere, if you make it clear that they are making up the difference in retirement funding.

Another option to consider for business based retirement accounts is a SIMPLE IRA. Similar to a SEP, SIMPLE IRA's allow for income-deferred retirement funding like a Traditional IRA. Where the SEP and SIMPLE IRA's differ is that SEPs are based on a percent of income while a SIMPLE is capped to deferral limits in dollars. Both require employee matches, but SIMPLEs match what the employee puts in of their own money. They are a little more complex to maintain than a SEP, because there are more moving parts with employee contributions.

The final option to consider is the traditional 401k, (or 403b for not for profit organizations). These were originally designed for larger companies with 20 or more employees and have larger limits for deferrals than SIMPLE IRAs. The company can also choose whether or not to have a match each year based on company profits. These plans can be the most expensive to set up and maintain, however, so you need to consider the benefits you would gain from the plan when choosing which is best for you.

There are some intricacies involved with some retirement options that allow employee participation, including a requirement on the percent of employees that have to contribute each year for the plan to remain in existence. There are many financial planners who specialize in business retirement options, and it is best to consult with one of them before making your final decision. If you don't have a financial planner readily available to you or haven't found one you particularly like, you can always contact a brokerage such as Vanguard or Fidelity, and they can walk you through some of your options as well.

Business Image

Physical Image

Every entrepreneur's business will have both a physical and non-physical (online) image, and this is something that should be actively maintained. The kind of things that make up your business's physical image include your building, staff, business cards and other marketing collateral such as brochures and pamphlets, uniforms, etc. Basically anything that can be held, felt, or seen without a computer makes up your physical image.

We discussed previously the location idea; however, if you do decide to get an actual space to work out of, it is important that it gives the right impression to your clientele. If you work in a blue-collar industry, you don't want to show too much opulence or you may have a problem connecting with your staff or customers. In the same respect, too nice of a location for an accounting firm, for example, might make people wonder about where your fees are going rather than give the impression that you manage money well.

As far as employees and uniforms go, it is crucial to have an employee handbook defining what kind of business you are running to clear up any potential misconceptions that employees may have about what's allowed and what isn't. If you hire lawn care workers, do you want them wearing anything they want with holes or profanity, or do you want them wearing your branded t-shirts? In the same respect, is it okay for an employee to smoke in front of clients

Business Image

or smell of smoke while greeting people as your receptionist, or do you prefer for new clients to not have that as their first impression of your organization? It is amazing what people think is acceptable as an employee if you don't take the time to set these expectations.

Employee handbooks go even further than just looks and smells of employees but also addresses actions. Do you want a company that allows your sales rep's to show up late to client meetings or to arrive at a customer's to cut their lawn at 7am the next day because they got behind the days before? Your policies in place should include how your employees should represent themselves to the community, as well as steps to correct actions that go against the corporate culture you are creating.

Another big part of your physical image is your business card. It sounds shallow, but people draw a lot of conclusions about you from your business card – especially in the networking arena. A business card should be thick enough to not be confused with a sheet of copy paper or a sticker, but not so thick that you could use it to prop open a door in an emergency. It typically will contain the following information: your business name, a logo, a slogan, your name, your title, and your contact information.

In deconstructing your business card, let's begin with the logo. Your logo can initially be designed by working with a print shop, an independent graphic designer, or using an online service such as 99designs to create your logo. I personally like having more than one set of eyes on the idea in logo development, so I recommend using 99designs or a similar service. It allows many designers to get a crack at your logo and allows you to fully engage in the creative process, because you see multiple options and can even ask the designers to merge two or three ideas into one.

One of the first times that I had to use a designer to create a business card, they asked me a lot of questions about the image I wished to portray as well as any symbols I could think of that related

Enough Dreaming

to my field. I then had to look online for additional examples to provide them, to give them a point of reference. What I got back in return was essentially the same card that I had already shown them, along with a couple variations on images that I suggested. It was good, but not great. The next time around, I used a service that had many designers instead of just one. I had to write up what's called a creative brief that described my company, who I was going to be servicing, and any existing materials that I might have that needed to be matched. Instead of asking for examples or images they simply asked for what kinds of images I liked as far as agricultural, or healthcare, or technology. The results were night and day. The members of this group each provided a different direction with the business card and logo, and it showed me some ideas that I didn't even know you could do. The experience resulted in a finished product that I liked much more.

In addition to the logo, your business card may need a slogan depending on your business name. If your business name is Jack's Auctions you are probably okay without having a slogan, but if your name is Clack and Frack Brothers, you might want to consider adding somewhere that you specialize in moving services.

Lastly, the final parts of a business card are your name, title, and contact information. If you have just begun an organization, you may wonder what title to use. I recommend something that involves leadership but doesn't necessarily state ownership. If you put owner on a card, it doesn't mean much because the word owner has a connotation that you are a one-man show that is just concerned with pulling profits out of the company. Instead consider using a title such as CEO, Principal, President, etc. This tells people that you most likely have an equity position in the company and you are the person who can call the shots and make deals. Also, when it comes to contact information, definitely have an email address that is registered to your website like john@frickandfrack.com and include your cell phone. Until your gross revenue is over $500,000 per year, you need to be as accessible as possible, and the email address shows that you are a legitimate company and not a fly-by-night organization.

Online Image

An entrepreneur's online image is comprised of your business website in addition to any comments that may be made about you on other sites, as well as your staff's online profiles. To start, you will need to register your website through a hosting company. This website can be either your name or what you do or both. For example, if your name is Frick and Frack, LLC, you may want to register frickandfrack.com and a name that goes along with what you do – moving services. So if you live in Atlanta, you might want to register something like altantamovingservice.com along with frickandfrack.com and then have the frickandfrack.com point or redirect to atlantamovingservice.com. By doing this, your website will come up when people search "Atlanta moving services" or "moving services in Atlanta" much more often since your URL or website name is one of the key elements of search engine optimization. Your website can be simple and list such things as your services, your prices, your contact information, and the areas where you provide service, if it is limited. You also need to be concerned with what comes up in a search for your company when people are looking for you and your company online. The best way to approach this is to be involved in social media outlets.

There are many online sites you can build for your company that will provide additional benefits to your primary website. You should have a business and a personal account on such websites as Facebook, Twitter, Instagram, LinkedIn, and Pinterest. You can also set up business specific sites and register your company on other review sites like Yelp, Angie's List, and anything else that may be industry specific. As you grow your business, getting clients and customers to post positive reviews on these sites will help your on-

Enough Dreaming

line image and reputation and lessen the impact of the occasional negative review that may pop up from either a dissatisfied customer or even vindictive competitors.

As online reputation websites have emerged, they have become both a blessing and a curse to many businesses. For a new business, having many positive comments can help to speed up the natural word of mouth referrals that develop over time, as people will be more likely to try a business that is "vouched for" online. Unfortunately, competitors can also take advantage of your online reputation page by posting unwarranted negative reviews to try to draw potential customers away. This is a well-known issue that many of these review sites are trying to combat while keeping in mind the actual customer's first amendment rights. The best thing to do with your online reputation pages is to be as proactive as possible about getting your customers to put positive reviews on the site. Whether negative reviews are written by actual customers or vindictive competitors, having a plethora of positive reviews to combat the handful of negative ones is the best course of action.

As you build your team, you should also encourage employees to have business profiles online if they have any interactions with your client base. No one wants to have an employee searched and a negative impression given to potential customers to the point where they begin to distrust your decision making in hiring such a person.

Trademarks, Copyrights, Patents, and Secure Email

In the same way that entrepreneurs will want to protect themselves from online searching, they should also protect their company legally by registering trademarks, copyrights, and having security in place for communication by way of a secured email address. By registering your trademark, it will keep competitors from creating similar logos that may confuse your clients and infringe on the brand you have developed. Similarly, copyrighting anything that is proprietary to your company is equally important in securing your position in a market. Patents will also come into play if you are creating products for which you can get both design and utility patents that prevent others from making similar looking or functioning products for a period of time. These patents add value to your company in the long run and become an asset that is purchasable by others who may like the specifics of how you create a product. If you secure a patent on your process or product, other companies may wish to purchase the ability to use this through a method called licensing. If you license your product or process to a company, they agree to pay you a fee for all of their products they produce using your proprietary method. Lastly, a secured email address that is created through your website prevents hackers from being able to get the information as easily. No one wants to email you their credit card information or anything sensitive to an AOL or Gmail account, because they aren't sure who else may be able to gain access to that information in the future.

Strategic Management

Core Value & Mission Statement

It is very important for every entrepreneur to take the time to put together a mission statement for the business as well as assign some core values, even if you start off as a sole proprietorship. These things will help provide focus in the future when making decisions as to how to expand and what employees may be a good fit for hiring.

Mission statements typically state what the business does and provide the overall direction of the business. For example, instead of stating something like, "Our mission is to mow lawns and trim trees for the local community," it should be more defined as to why you are doing what you are doing, or your passion. For example, "Our mission is to serve our community with timely and respectful landscaping maintenance through competitive and full-service packages." This defines the overall approach to lawns very differently. This mission statement means that you will be vigilant about working around the time needs of customers and that you will only have respectful staff who treats each house as if it was their own. Also, by including such words as competitive and full-service, it means that you offer prices that match or are close to what others in the industry offer. These words also lead someone to believe that perhaps you have other partners with whom you have worked out agreements, so you can do everything for clients on the surface such as tree trimming, planting new shrubs, and maintaining irrigation systems. By doing this, you are able to act and perform as a full-service company instead of a single guy with a lawnmower.

Mission statements can also involve secondary passions that you may wish to integrate into your business in addition to your primary aspect of cutting lawns, in this example. For instance, perhaps you have a passion for serving people who are out of work or single mothers who find it hard to maintain a house plus take care of their children. In these cases your mission statements may be more along the lines of, "Our mission is to provide hope to others through lifestyle based lawn care which empowers individuals through employment and child care support." By creating a mission statement such as this, it will provide guidance to an entrepreneur as to what type of person they might wish to hire in the future – someone with a compelling story of hardship. This could also provide an avenue to do marketing – such as single mom's groups and mom support services, and could give guidance as to an appropriate name – such as Employment Lawn Services.

Core values support the mission statement by giving specific guidelines that you are looking to acquire or aspire to have in the future. Some examples of these might be, "We believe in serving our community and treating every home as if they are our own;" "We believe in creating opportunities to empower individuals though steady employment;" "We believe in good stewardship and taking care of our clients, our equipment, and our coworkers;" or "We believe in making every effort to accommodate our customers' schedules, even if it inconveniences ourselves in doing so."

By putting these core values together, it provides three things that companies don't have naturally without them. First, it provides future direction and movement so you know where to put your efforts. Second, it provides employees with a clear expectation of the job before they are even hired. Someone who understands these core values beforehand may understand why they have to go to a different location other than the closest one, because the closest one has a newborn napping during the time you were about to be at their house mowing. Thirdly, it provides what is known as, to marketers, a point of differentiation. It is a marketable tool that sets your business apart from your competitors and gives you a publishable tool for your website and a brochure, if you choose to create one.

SWOT Analysis

The SWOT analyses can be found in a business plan, but they can also be done on their own as a global analysis of what's going on inside and outside of the company. SWOT stands for Strengths, Weaknesses, Opportunities, and Threats. Strengths and weaknesses are from the standpoint of within the company, while opportunities and threats are seen as market specific. For example, this could be how a typical SWOT is written:

Strengths

Strong Leadership

Quick Response Times on Customer Service

95% Sales Acquisition Rate

Weaknesses

Inflexible Pricing Structure

Below Average Profit Margins

High Employee Turnover

Opportunities

Strategic Management

New Market Share Available

Upcoming Legislation

Partnership Opportunity

Threats

Low Market Barriers to Entry

Known Competitor Stealing Employees

Upcoming Hurricane Season

The most frequent question that people have when creating a SWOT analysis is: how do I know if something is one category or another because it could be both? For example, if there is upcoming legislation that might affect your business, you need to consider if it will make things better or worse. If it could be even better, then the legislation would be an opportunity, but if not, it would be classified as a threat. Sometimes there are two separate outcomes possible from the same event which can be simultaneously an opportunity and a threat. In this case, list the event individually in both correct columns.

Similarly, strengths can often be the opposites of our weaknesses as most people realize. Someone who has a strong work ethic could also be challenged that they have a weak work-life balance. When doing this analysis, you can list them in both sides, but what is more beneficial is to weigh both sides and determine which is most true. Does working 12 hours a day give your business a competitive edge because everyone is outworking the competition, or does this simply add to the reasons why you have high employee turnover?

Enough Dreaming

The exercise of completing a SWOT analysis is extremely important for any company looking to grow. The key component in completing a SWOT analysis is blatant honesty. It won't help your company at all if people agree that your hard driving personality is a strength when all they do is complain about it at home. In the same way, don't say that your company's weakness is high expenses when you pay yourself well over the market average and intentionally use the business bank account as your personal piggy bank. If you do these kinds of things while creating your SWOT analysis, you will not only hinder your business growth but you can also ingrain these bad traits as facts instead of fixable qualities.

Competitive Analyses

Competitive analyses are done once a business becomes large enough that the competitive atmosphere is truly affecting the potential of the business's long term growth. That said, many companies think they should do a competitive analysis right away because competitors exist, but the reality is that most small businesses can grow to be a lifestyle business for a few employees fairly easily without concerning yourself with competitors. This is due to the fact that there are a lot of businesses in every industry that aren't getting exactly what they want from their existing vendors. By simply keeping your nose to the ground and working hard to put together something people like, you should be able to grow your business without really concerning yourself with your competitors. Now, once a business is large enough that competitors are starting to take notice, and you need to refine your organization so that they can't take your market share easily, a competitive analysis is necessary.

A competitive analysis looks at competitors through the eyes of the 7 P's of Marketing. These are qualities of a business that were originally defined by Neil Borden and have been expanded upon over time. These qualities are Product, Price, Place, Promotion, Packaging, Positioning, and People. If we examine the core business and competitors through these qualities, it reveals an accurate landscape of growth opportunity.

I have found that there is a slight difference between a product industry and a service industry in using the 7 P's for analysis. In the case of products, price is how much your service is going for as well as how much the cost is to produce the good. Place is in reference to where the goods are being sold and in what geographical areas. Promotion refers to what marketing or advertising is being done as well as any cross-promotional work between two products in a larger organization. Packaging refers to the actual packaging of the product that makes you understand how it is to be used. Positioning refers to what space the company is in within a market – whether it is high-end luxury or low-end low margin. People refers to what assets in leadership or staff the company possesses. Finally, product of course, references the goods being sold.

In the service industry, these are slightly changed. The product category is really more of an "S" for service, as in, what is being provided to customers. The price is how much is being charged for what amount of service, since service products are typically contingent on either time or area. Place can be used to detail where the services are being sold or distributed, but more often it is more important that place stand for where the services are being rendered. Promotion is similar in that promotion includes how services are being promoted through marketing channels. Packaging isn't a physical packaging as much as the perception of the company. Perception is the cover to your service as much as the packaging is for products. Positioning is similar, whether the company is going after high-end customers or low-end customers. This is more fluid for service industries, however, because making a change only requires changing where time is being spent, and not the re-engineering of a product. And lastly People can be even more important for a service industry as people are the ones directly providing the connection to your customers. For a more in-depth look at this area, I recommend looking at The Marketing Mix chapter within the *Harvard Business Review*.

The bottom line concern when considering completing a competitive analysis is for you to keep your metrics the same throughout your analysis. By keeping this lens continuity, you can more easily see the gaps in the coverage offered by your competitors. By positioning your business in this space it will present the most amount of growth for the least amount of effort within your competitive landscape.

Growth Strategies

Online Growth and Branding

Online growth is extremely important for every business whether you have an online e-commerce business or a government contracted business; if you don't have an online presence you are missing out on opportunities. While it is more obvious that if you can sell your products over the Internet you would need online growth, there are many businesses that are acquired and completed in a face to face fashion. Your online presence adds or detracts from your business's brand.

Your business brand is how your organization is perceived by your market and your community. Your brand is shaped through every interaction a person has with your organization. It is globally comprised of all the images associated with your organization including your logo, business card, marketing collateral, website, as well as the interactions that you and your staff have with the community and customers. Those are the things that you can control around your brand. Public relations often involve trying to use the community's interactions with your business in a positive way. That includes online responses to reviews as well as the reviews themselves, and any community events you may involve the business in. Without a conscious effort to shape your brand, the image given to the community will be created organically. Organic brand development typically includes highly positive interactions and highly negative ones since these are the only two types that generate word of mouth marketing on their own.

Your online representation is an important way for an organization to not only grow, but to also shape your online presence further. The ways that a business should use the online space are to have an appropriate and robust website showcasing your organization and to also have such things as informational articles and blogs. Blogs are articles that you write online about certain areas of your business, or the market, that people may want to know more about. These showcase your expertise in an area as well as provide the community with an image that you want to present.

Additional ways to engender online growth include registering online with geolocation services and review sites such as Google maps and Yelp. By doing these things, you can make your company more visible to people trying to find you while controlling your online image. If a negative review is posted online you can then typically respond to it if you are registered with the site, but more importantly, you can encourage customers to go online and post positive reviews about their experiences with your company that provide the community with a more accurate picture of your organization's product and services.

By actively engaging in online growth strategies and brand shaping activities, you will find that your company's growth will become amplified. Customers and business partners who do their due diligence about your business will find themselves positively reaffirmed in their desire to do business with you, and your market footprint will only expand.

Horizontal vs. Vertical Integration

Horizontal and vertical integration reference the industry in which your business resides. If you own a computer repair company servicing small businesses and you want to consider vertically integrating, you can look at your existing clients and perhaps offer additional services to the same group. Instead of just offering computer repair services, you can expand your offerings to include software development, website development, or equipment leasing for small businesses.

Horizontal integration for a business includes taking the same service offerings and expanding into new industries. For example, the same computer repair business may wish to expand by integrating into consumer based computer repair services with a storefront or into large company computer repair services that offer a more robust service line to meet the needs of a large company.

Often, businesses try to expand their services or products horizontally because they think that it takes less effort, but the reality is that you can often grow vertically more easily than horizontally because you have an existing client base that you can work off of. By interviewing your current client or customer base, you can frequently discover opportunities in the market. These opportunities allow you to either consider vertically integrating into this space, or show you the opportunity to provide your customer with a referral to a partner organization that may reciprocate with business to your organization in the future.

Formal & Informal Partnerships

Formal and informal partnerships are a crucial part of growing and sustaining a small business. These partnerships provide your organization with the sustainability of a much larger organization while being more of a "value add" to your clients and customers. To give an example, if you are in the computer repair business, you may discover that some of the other needs your clients have are in the IT space, or equipment leasing, banking, marketing, accounting, etc. By having all of these other spaces identified with business partners, you are able to do two things. First, you can be more of a resource for your customers when those needs come up. Over time your clients may come to you for a recommendation of who can provide the services they need. If they need a good accountant and you have someone in mind that meets their needs, by giving that referral, it strengthens the relationship you have with the client yourself, as well as your relationship with the referral partner. In turn, they very well might refer customers to you that need computer repair services. Secondly, by having referral partners it provides you with allies within your client's organization. The next time they mention to their IT provider a project that has computer needs, the IT company, one of your referral partners, is more likely to recommend they speak with you about these needs rather than the IT company doing it themselves or recommending a competitor.

By positioning your business as the best referring entity for your clients you are able to provide them with a whole level of services that your competitors might not have. Not only will you be able to satisfy their needs, you can build your business by having referrals given back to you from the company you referred to. Clients tend to prefer word of mouth referrals because there is some accountability in place. If the person they were referred to knows that a lead came from a good referral source instead of an ad or the internet, they are more likely to provide top notch service because they could potentially fracture a referral relationship and lose future business. Some companies do not like to provide referrals for this exact reason out of fear that it may come back and make them look bad; however, if you do your due diligence and check out your potential referral partners online and get some client recommendations, you will find that these partnership growth opportunities well outweigh the risk associated with them.

Another way that businesses create partnerships is through formal arrangements. Some partnering organizations have structures already in place for fee-based referrals as a way to entice business relationships. If a larger company already has a budget of $100,000 for business development, they often have an affiliate marketing program approved where you can refer a client to them and get money back in turn for the referral. Personally, I don't like these kinds of relationships because you lose out on all the long-term benefits of the referral. Without the accountability, these referrals are more likely to make everyone look bad in the long run.

Networking

Networking is a great way for entrepreneurs to create partnerships. The most common type of networking involves being a part of a group, club, or association. This type of group will put on networking events that allow you to give a 30 second pitch to others about your products and services, and perhaps you find a good match for your organization. I consider this passive networking since all the legwork is done by the organization hosting the event. Overall, this kind of marketing is fairly unbeneficial. Frequently you will find the people who attend these events to be the sales agents for a larger company and therefore don't have the ability to cater to your clients as well as you want them to.

A better type of networking to consider is active networking. Once you secure your first client or customer, you should proactively ask them which vendors they consider to be a real asset to them. Once you have this information, make the point of introducing yourself to the company, share the fact that you both have a mutual client or customer in this person, and then make a point to meet up with them to explain your products and services while learning about theirs. If you continue to actively do this with your clients or customers as well as with their preferred vendors, you will eventually root out all the best product or service providers within your industry. These are the types of people and organizations that you will want to consider partnering with in referral partnerships. They will yield the best results for your clients and customers while making your business look good.

Enough Dreaming

Time Management

Time management is one of the most challenging aspects for many entrepreneurs. You frequently have to put in 80 hour work weeks to create and grow a company. The key in maximizing your time is time management. You should have a plan of action and stick to it religiously or you will find your days getting away from you. The best overall guidelines to make are that from 8am-5pm is your time to get the work done, and from 7am-8am and 5pm-7pm is your time to plan, grow, and do operational tasks such as bookkeeping. While you are growing your business, you will need to meet with people during business hours to either make sales to customers or clients, or to meet with potential business partners. The best way to do this is to block certain times during the week and try to stick to only allowing a couple of these in any week. For example, you might tentatively keep open Tuesday through Thursday lunch hours as well as a 10am and 3pm coffee slot on those days. Once two of these times are filled you move on to the following week and fill those because the current week is "closed". By keeping a schedule like this, you will find you still have plenty of time to get the work done needed to keep your existing clients and customers happy, while having enough availability to meet people to grow your business.

If you keep your calendar regimented in this kind of fashion, it will keep you from getting too tied up in non-money-generating activities while keeping cash flow a priority. In the event that you need to meet with more and more clients or customers during business hours, you can consider expanding by hiring help. Until this time comes, however, hiring someone would be more of a luxury than a necessity for your business.

Two of the things that I had to learn the hard way was how to manage my time correctly on the phone as well as how to keep up with my emails. When it came to phone calls, I believed that every call that wasn't a telemarketer was worth taking because I assumed that every interaction represented an opportunity that I might miss out on if I didn't make myself available. What I learned instead is that important conversations will always happen eventually and that all the non-essential calls will fall by the wayside. My particular method of choice was to put my phone on silent with no vibrate when I started working on a project, and I could only check it and answer the truly urgent text messages every half an hour. Phone messages could be checked after an hour but I couldn't return the non-urgent calls until either the project was done or until the end of the day. By treating phone calls in this manner, I was able to maintain a laser focus on my tasks and get more done in a day than most of my peers.

I took a similar approach to emails as I did to phone calls. What I learned was that in the corporate world, emails and texts have become interchangeable so where in the past you might take 20 or 30 minutes writing a well crafted email, now you need only a minute to respond with simple texted questions, and this could easily set off a reaction of 30 emails back and forth. What you have to understand is that it is generally more important for you to complete the tasks on hand than to communicate with other people incessantly throughout the day. I had a friend who would work Monday through Thursday on projects and Friday was his day to make phone calls and respond to his inbox full of emails. By implementing this method he was more productive than his partners who frequently worked 60-hour work-weeks, and yet was still able to leave for home by 5pm each day.

Resources

There is one key ingredient in being able to successfully navigate the entrepreneurial waters, and that is constant professional growth. There is a saying that goes "you don't know what you don't know." As long as you are in the constant pursuit of the unknown, you will find yourself successful in business growth.

Enough Dreaming

One of the best ways for entrepreneurs to grow is through professional resources. Frequently, industry associations or trade journals can provide entrepreneurs with ideas on business expansion and market needs. In addition, there are many resources that help entrepreneurs on how to run, manage, and expand their own businesses. These resources include such things as the Small Business Association, Entrepreneur Magazine, and Inc. Magazine. In addition to these, there are a variety of very good books available at local bookstores or Amazon that can be very informational. Most of the books, however, tend to be centered around certain areas of business such as marketing, management, or leadership, so you need to have an idea of what areas are the most important for your organization before deciding which to purchase.

Exit Strategies

Selling a Business

Most entrepreneurs have the dream of building their business and eventually selling it to fund their retirement or their next project. What you need to know, if this is your goal, are the three most common ways that businesses are typically valued: asset-based, market-based, and revenue-based. There are other variations depending on your industry but these three should provide a global overview of the valuation process.

Asset-Based Valuations

Asset-based valuations are when you take all the tangible assets that a business has accumulated over time and put a price on it. The theory behind asset-based valuations is to ask this question: How much would it take for someone to build this business on their own? The typical assets that are factored into such a valuation are the assets listed on the books (such as equipment, real estate, office furniture, accounts receivables) as well as the more subjective assets such as customer lists, existing contracts and the values they bring, in addition to such things as patents, trademarks, branding and goodwill. This kind of valuation is seen predominately in commodity based businesses where someone is going to pay you for the effort of putting everything together instead of looking at what the business produces.

Market-Based Valuations

Market-based valuations are more in line with how you would do a real estate valuation. You take a market snapshot and compare the asking price or the offer to what other comparable businesses in the same market with the same footprint of revenue, liability, and assets are currently being offered for or have sold for. Frequently this type of valuation is used as a check after another type of valuation is used to set the asking price.

Revenue-Based Valuations

Revenue-based valuation is one of the most common types of valuations. What it essentially does is to look at the current bottom-line revenue the business has had historically, and then extrapolate into the future what the predicted revenue will be. The current revenue's multiplier to determine value involves an estimate of the risk involved. This determination of risk involves looking at many different factors such as the size of the business, how diversified your referral sources are, where your business is coming from, how stable the business seems given the market and legislative environment, and if the owners and leadership of the company are going to stay involved with the business after the sale. Multipliers typically range between 2 and 7 times the bottom line profit for a business using this method.

Professional valuation experts use all of these types of valuations plus others. In the event that you are considering a buyout strategy, you may wish to consult with one of these experts in your area for advice on best positioning your company for acquisition.

Using a Business as a Launch Pad

One of the best uses of a start-up business is to use it as a launch pad for future career growth. Many entrepreneurial ventures are considered lifestyle businesses that don't accumulate enough in sales or assets to be acquired by another person or funded by investors, but that doesn't mean it isn't a worthwhile venture. Lifestyle businesses essentially give entrepreneurs the ability to work for themselves and produce an income directly from their efforts. For many people, it offers the ability to gain career skills that wouldn't be possible through a larger company for many years such as bookkeeping, management, sales, and operations management. It is not uncommon for people looking for rapid growth in their careers to start their own businesses and transition to a larger company in the future by gaining massive amounts of experience. Whether you are currently unemployed and looking for work or recently graduated from school, starting your own business shows initiative and frequently sky rockets your future career success in a relatively short amount of time.

Summary

Being an entrepreneur is an honorable career choice but it is not for the faint of heart. If you are ambitious, have the energy to continuously learn, and have good advisors who you surround yourself with, you will have the greatest chance of success.

The overall steps to starting a business are:

- Organize your business through your chosen legal structure
- Create a business plan to best position your company for success in the market
- Know your operations thoroughly, minimize your costs, and maximize your efforts in the most profitable areas
- Keep accurate records for bookkeeping and organizational analysis
- Determine your team of advisors to help you along the way including an accountant and lawyer
- Sell, Sell, Sell
- Continuously Learn

If you follow these seven basic steps you can set yourself up for entrepreneurial success.

Summary

Index

Getting Started 7
Mousetrap 2.0   8

Business Plan 18
Business Plan Example   19
Business Plan Breakdown   32

Defining a Business 40
Types of Businesses   43
    Sole Proprietorships   43
    Partnerships   44
    Corporations   45

Operational Management 49
Accounting   49
    Bookkeeping   60
    Financial Statements   62

Index

Balance Sheets	62
Income Statements	63
Statement of Cash Flows	64
Statement of Retained Earnings	64
Human Resources	65
Appropriate Classification of Workers	66
Fair Labor Standards	68
Hiring	69
Firing	74
Banking	77
Secured Loans vs Unsecured Loans	78
Real Estate	79
Retirement	81

Business Image *84*

Physical Image	84
Online Image	87
Trademarks, Copyrights, Patents, and Secure Email	88

Strategic Management *90*

| Core Value & Mission Statement | 90 |
| SWOT Analysis | 92 |

Competitive Analyses   94

Growth Strategies *97*

Online Growth and Branding   97
Horizontal vs. Vertical Integration   98
Formal & Informal Partnerships   99
Networking   101
Time Management   102
Resources   103

Exit Strategies *105*

Selling a Business   105
    Asset-Based Valuations   105
    Market-Based Valuations   106
    Revenue-Based Valuations   106
Using a Business as a Launch Pad   107

Summary *108*